MANAGING THE SITE

JOHN CORLESS

A practical guide to managing a construction site in Ireland.

Thanks to The Health & Safety Authority for permission to reproduce certain information contained in this book and for their co-operation generally.

Thanks also to Ms. Noreen Linehan and Construction Accessories Ltd. for their support and commitment to this publication.

– John Corless

MANAGING THE SITE

A guide to managing a construction site in Ireland.

By John Corless

MANAGING THE SITE

© John Corless

First published 2006.
Sionnach Media,
47 Grace Park Meadows, Drumcondra, Dublin 9, Ireland.
www.sionnach-media.com

A catalogue record for this title is
available from the British Library.

ISBN-13: 978-0-9553804-0-2
ISBN-10: 0-9553804-0-5

Printed in Ireland by ColourBooks Ltd., Baldoyle Industrial Estate, Dublin 13.

DECLARATION

The publishers have made every effort to ensure that the information contained in this book is correct at the time of going to press. All recommendations are made without guarantee on the part of the author and the publishers. The author and publishers disclaim any liability for damages or injury resulting from the use of this information.

CONTENTS

Chapter 1 – THE ROLE OF THE SITE MANAGER

1.1   Aims and Limitations of This Book

This book is aimed at Site Managers working in the construction industry in Ireland, and those who aspire to, or considering, this challenging position. The book brings together the many aspects of this job, but deals with them from the Site Manager's viewpoint. In-company training manuals outline how the job should be done from the company's perspective. This book is different in that it recognises that the Site Manager can't always do things the way that employers may desire. Usually it's not that simple. Judgement calls have to be made, and influencing factors impact in ways that make the proposed company standpoint impossible to implement.   It's in these situations that the Site Manager has to 'call-it' – and this is where this book can help. *Managing The Site* sets out to illustrate to the Site Manager the factors that should influence the decisions made and the impact one decision or judgement call can have on another.   It also suggests ways of minimizing the time spent on the myriad of paperwork circulating around most sites, without neglecting important record-keeping duties.

The book doesn't cover everything; and aspects are treated differently.   Equally, not all Site Managers will apply the advice offered in the exact way that it is outlined here. There are parts that will appear to some to be unnecessary; other parts may seem childishly simple. There are those to whom this book will be a great help; others may find parts very complicated.

A few quick points need to be made before we go any further.

One of the great deficiencies of the English language is the absence of a sexless term of reference covering both "he" and "she." A sort of a personalised form of "it." Throughout this book I have constantly and consistently referred to the Site Manager as "he." This term, in the absence of a more suitable one, is intended to cover both sexes. It is not intended as a sexist term in any way.

Head Office. Most Site Managers operate as independently as possible from their bosses at head office or other wings of the company located there. From time to time the term "head office" appears in this text as a global term for those who work there, bosses and colleagues alike.

Now on to the obvious question.

1.2   Why Would Anyone Want To Be A Site Manager?

Why would anyone want to be a Site Manager? Why bother? What is it that attracts some people to management positions? Before we get into this book let's explore a few of these reasons why anyone would want to be a Site Manager.

- Salary
- Status
- Authority
- Leadership
- Ambition

Firstly, while the job pays well, if it's only the money you're after, you'll be better paid in some trades than you will as a Site Manager. If you are a top earning carpenter, bricklayer or electrician you might find that the Site Manager has to survive on lower wages than your existing salary. Sorry to disappoint you on that one.

Secondly, if you pursue status, you might find other industries hold more prestige than the humble construction industry. There isn't much status in evidence on most building sites. But of course status is relative, so perhaps the Site Managers job may offer prestige to some.

If you crave authority I suggest you seek medical advice, take up sports refereeing, or seek a post with your Local Corporation or council, sticking parking tickets on illegally parked cars! You will find a considerable authority deficit in site management.

If you are a natural leader it will help you as a Site Manager, but as you sit in the office for hours at meetings or dealing with paperwork, you'll need all your leadership skills to guide yourself through the day.

Ambitious? Some successful Site Managers do go on to become Contracts Mangers or Contracts Directors. The job can be another rung on the ladder for those seeking high office. The majority, however, remain as Site Managers.

Yet many people are attracted to the job. It certainly offers responsibility and there is a certain feeling of pride to be gained from managing the building of a project. Despite what the designers may think, the Site Manager has a huge role to play in the way a building turns out, apart from the obvious effects of high or low quality finishes delivered. The Site Manager will have the designer's ear to make subtle suggestions that may have a very tangible effect on the end product.

1.3   What Exactly Is The Role of The Site Manager?

This book looks at the role of the Site Manager in considerable detail. It discusses the tasks and situations that he will find himself in, on a daily basis. But before we go any further, we will define the underlying role of the Site Manager.

The role or function of the Site Manager is to deliver:

A **Quality** Project
On **Time**
On **Budget**
Safely.

These are the four key issues: quality, time, budget and safety. The Site Manager cannot ignore any one of these key elements. The balancing of the four points will present the most challenges to the Site Manager in the course of his working day. It's very easy to get three out of four; two out of four can be done without a Site Manager at all, and one out of four will happen almost by itself. But getting the four key ingredients included is the core reason that the Site Manager is there in the first place.

Anyone can get the job built on time if he has an unlimited budget or doesn't have to worry about quality or safety. Equally if the budget is tight, the job can be built if safety and quality are sacrificed. Similarly if time is not an issue, then quality and safety can be second to none. It's the gelling together of the four key functions which determines the success or failure of the job, and ultimately, of the Site Manager.

In this book we examine these four key factors and the little things that make them up. Every topic covered in this publication relates in some way or another to these key points. Paperwork and record keeping for example is part of the make up of quality, safety and budget. People management is about all four of the key elements of site management.

The Site Manager is frequently promoted or appointed without proper training, yet is expected to know what he should be doing once in the job, and may get a ticking off (to put it mildly) when he hasn't done it. This book aims to explain many of the tasks the Site Manager is expected to perform, and also to explain why these tasks are important within the organisation of the job and the firm for which he works.

1.4　Site Manager's Responsibilities

The Site Manager is responsible for getting the job done. To do this he must have a positive "can do" attitude, must be able to delegate work, and have the ability to remain focused.

The Site Manager should be a good planner and be a good communicator. He must have the ability to identify and review all the available options, and must be decisive. He has to protect the interests of his employers at all times. He must control and administer the resources on site and maintain continuity of work. All of these individual requirements are dealt with in the relevant sections of this book.

1.5　Demands on the Site Manager

The Site Manager must balance the various demands on his time carefully. While head office would probably wish that he lived on the job, and thought of nothing else but his employers, the Site Manager has to factor-in all the other demands on his time. There's more to life than work - and nobody - site managers included - should ever lose sight of that point.

Demands on the Site Manager include the demands of the job itself – having to turn up and spend his time there, and deal with the daily tasks involved in getting the job built. Head office will also impose demands and satisfying their requirements and keeping them off his back can be a challenge. The Site Manager has to have quality time available for his family and should maintain interests outside work.

The location and physical characteristics of the site (as opposed to the job itself) may pose demands on the Site Manager. It may be a long way from his home requiring him to relocate or "live out of a suitcase" in bed and breakfast or rented temporary accommodation. The Site Manager may be extremely tired from patrolling the various ongoing sections if the site is a large one. This is especially the case in wet weather during the groundworks phase of site work.

The requirements of the client will have to be balanced with head office's demands for expediency and profit. The Site Manager may wish to do the job a totally different way, were he given that freedom. Sometimes suppressing his wishes and accommodating a blend of the others can be a difficult balancing act.

Health problems or ongoing illness will have a huge impact on the Site Manager's performance.

Ambition is another great pressure or distraction for managers in any industry. While some managers are quite content to just get on with the job, others are constantly looking for promotional opportunities – often to the determent of their performance on the current project. Chapter 12 of this book is devoted entirely to career management.

The effective management of sub-contractors is one of the great challenges for site management personnel. The Site Manager must be able to withstand the seemingly petty nature of their complaints as they test his mental strength. Sub contractors are dealt with in detail in Chapter 8.

The interaction with co-workers can put a lot of pressure on the Site Manager. Company or site politics, especially in medium or larger companies can be a huge distraction, adding to the busy Site Manager's already long list of worries.

Availability of materials may seem an unlikely source of pressure on the Site Manager at first, but any difficulties will have a bearing on progress, and add to the worries of the Site Manager.

Site access issues raised by narrow roads or dangerous junctions or traffic restrictions cause headaches for the Site Manager. On sites located on busy city streets this can be a major issue dominating work scheduling every day throughout the job. Transport too may be an issue. The site may be located in an area where there is extremely heavy traffic or on a busy road or a clearway – placing greater demands on the Site Manager than normal.

Neighbours may need regular appeasing and/or may be extremely difficult to deal with. They may have genuine complaints relating to noise or dust pollution, or they may be 'trying it on' with bogus complaints. Either way the Site Manager has to deal with it.

The design team too may cause problems for the Site Manager. They may be slow to issue information, or may be very picky – demanding an unreasonable standard of workmanship. A personality clash may develop between the Site Manager and their representatives. Again the Site Manager has to deal with it.

New technologies may challenge the Site Manager. New processes or materials may be introduced – ones that he may not have come across before, all adding to the pressure.

1.6   Demands On The Contractor

The contractor may have problems or challenges on a number of fronts. This site may be one of many ongoing simultaneously, all needing finance and attention and all making demands on head office management time.

Demands may include this particular site/project, other sites/jobs/projects, finance/cash flow – demands on money within the firm may place seemingly unreasonable demands and restrictions on the sites. Perhaps some other site is losing money and head office suddenly has to make savings across all sites.

Competitors too put pressure on each other. Tendering may have to be keener than normal – as a result the profit margin may be tighter and the performance of the site may have to be higher than previous levels.

Market forces will always influence contractors. Maybe the industry is slowing down or expanding rapidly. The firm may be under pressure to scale down or keep up. The effects can be wide ranging – with a surplus of personnel at one end of the scale to a complete drought of available resources when things are busy.

New technological developments may have huge cost implications or steep learning curves, adding to the pressure on the firm. Staff – union problems perhaps, or shortages due to expansion, or other personnel problems can be another source of discomfort for the contractor.

Planning & other government intervention – can have a huge impact on existing and proposed contracts and the geographic location of the firm's base in relation to the market opportunities can both put contractors under pressure.

Any one or number of underlying reasons may be behind problems on the site. Head office personnel may be behaving strangely when they come to site and the Site Manager may interpret this, as having something to do with him and/or the way the job is running, when in reality there is some external reason driving the strange behaviour. If one site is losing money for example, head office representatives may turn-up unexpectedly at a different site and demand that the manager make savings.

When head office representatives visit the site, the information and opinions gathered are later amalgamated with the information and opinions gathered on other sites, and any other relevant information, and the sum of all this data is frequently used to formulate policy. This new policy may be communicated to site with great urgency and may contradict the policy of the previous week or even the previous day. This reaction management style is all too common, but like everything else heaped upon him, it has to be managed by the Site Manager.

1.7   Manage The Problems

The Site Manager has to manage the problems that face him on a daily basis. He has to be able to foresee them, get around them and get on with the job. He can't go running to his superiors every time something goes wrong or things don't go his way. He has to manage the crisis.   Indeed, the more experienced the manager becomes, the less likely he will be, to involve head office in his problems and the less dependent he will be on them.

So what kind of problems can he expect? Once again we look at the key four ingredients. Quality, time, budget and safety. The quality may drop; he has to deal with it.   The work may be progressing slower than was planned. The Site Manager has to manage the problem. Costs may be escalating – he has to take action. Or there may be safety concerns to be dealt with. Again it is the Site Manager who has to deal with them.

Sometimes it will appear that there are ongoing contests or battles - "the site" versus "head office" or "the site" versus "other sites" for resources. Or "quality" versus "time," "safety" versus "time," "costs" versus "safety," etc. The Site Manager has to take all this in his stride, he has to "manage" these problems also.

1.8   Planning

I like the phrase from the autobiography of Roy Keane the international footballer: "Fail to plan - plan to fail."

Proper planning will prevent many problems. This involves planning the scheduling of tasks, delivery and storage of materials, and supervising the workers to ensure that safety, performance and quality, are delivered.

In the course of this book we will look at programming of works, scheduling of material, safety and quality as well as many other management functions.

Failure to properly plan can stem from any number if reasons. If the Site Manager is too busy dealing with current problems to look ahead, he will always have current problems.   If he doesn't have enough information he can't plan properly.   And if he is indecisive he has a major problem. The Site Manager has to be able to make decisions.   In addition he needs a sound knowledge of the industry and working practices and should never bluff when he is faced with new technologies or practices – pretending to be familiar with something he clearly isn't. His cover will be easily blown and his credibility damaged when it is.

1.9   Getting Ahead Of The Problem

Experience gained in the industry will stand greatly to the Site Manager as he goes about planning and scheduling work.   But how about work practices unfamiliar to the Site Manager?

One way to try and stay ahead of problems is called *tactical* or *scenario* planning. The – *What Happens If....* approach.   In other words, having a back-up plan or a number of back-up plans.

The *What Happens If....* style of planning is very useful and means that the thinking process has been carried *before* something goes wrong rather than *afterwards*. It should be a simple matter of implementing the back-up plan rather than trying to figure one out in the heat of the moment.

The Site Manager can prepare his *What Happens If......* plans around situations like drivers not turning-up for work, finishes to concrete surfaces not working out as well as hoped, etc. He can also apply this style of preparation to scheduling work, having a back-up plan if the weather forecasters got it wrong, or a sub-contractor fails to turn-up or deliver.

So many things can go wrong on a site that the Manager won't be able to do his *What happens if....* planning process for every eventuality, but he certainly should do it on the more probable events. Each work situation that the Site Manager finds himself in will present its own opportunities for scenario planning, and while he won't always have the answers – at least if something does go wrong – it shouldn't be a major surprise to him.

1.10   Delegation

The role of any manager is to get the job done through others. He is the team leader. Delegation is a very important element in management. Obviously the Site Manager will delegate the work on site, to the various trades and sub-contractors. But what about management functions? Some site management functions can be delegated and some can not, or at least *should* not.

The two essential elements in the delegation of management issues are ability and trust. There is no point in delegating a management role to someone who has no training or expertise in the particular field.

If, say, the delegation in question involves supervision of work; unless the person to whom the responsibility has been delegated, has some expertise in that particular work, how will he know if the job is done right?

The second point, trust, is a personal thing, and has to be built-up between the Site Manager and the other party involved. If the Site Manager asks say, a Site Engineer to check that pipes are laid to correct falls prior to backfilling – the Site Manager has to trust the engineer when he later confirms all is ok.

Expertise and trust are key elements of the delegation process and a reliable team will make the Site Manager's life a lot easier. The opposite will of course have the opposite effect.

1.11   The Can-Do Attitude

The "can-do" attitude is essential for the Site Manager. He can't let problems or situations get the better of him. He can't let pessimistic thinking prevail in nay situation. Certainly, difficulties should be recognised and not under-estimated, but they can't be allowed to dictate the pace of progress. Equally, the Site Manager can't let pessimism "creep-in" amongst workers and should involve them in devising "can-do" solutions to "can't-do" problems.

The Site Manager must face each situation with a "can-do" attitude. That is after all, what he is there for.

1.12 Controlling The Flow of Information

One of the most significant tasks the Site Manager has to carry-off is to control the flow of information outwards from the site. In the tactical battles that are fought daily, information flow is a very important weapon. This can involve information to client, designers, suppliers and even to head office. The tactical use of the various relevant documents available can be jeopardised by sporadic verbal or written communications from others on the site, giving the game away. To quote an example, if the Site Manager has decided for tactical reasons that he is not going to raise a specific item, say, absence of a dimension on a drawing, with the architect at this stage, the tactical benefits of this decision will be negated by a phone call or fax from the site engineer asking the question directly or in such another way as to highlight the requirement.

The Site Manager should devise a policy for the issuing of information from the site and should communicate this policy clearly to his colleagues on the site. This policy should be carefully followed when memos, faxes, e-mail or phone calls are to be initiated.

'Loose-talk' – breaches of the rules regarding the outward flow of information – should be dealt with speedily by the Site Manager to prevent recurrences, and to clearly highlight the importance of the policy.

1.13 It May Well End Up In Court.

The Site Manager should at all times keep in mind that actions he takes or fails to take while on the site may very well be decided upon in a court of law.

This is by no means an exaggeration. Many construction-related disputes end up in court or in arbitration. It might be a dispute with a supplier, a sub-contractor or the client. Perhaps it's as a result of an accident on the site. Whatever the reason the Site Manager may well be interrogated, maybe years later, on events that took place during his term in charge of the site.

The Site Manager must be mindful of this possibility as he goes about his daily duties in charge of the site. Whenever he is unsure of something, or when he feels uncomfortable about something, he should always ask himself: "How would this look in court?" It's a sobering thought and a good perspective from which to face each challenge.

Floorslab Accessories

- Continuous Hychair – various sizes
- Concrete Spacer blocks – double/triple cover
- Concrete Bars – 1 mtr long, various sizes
- Plastic tracking spacers – 25-50mm cover
- Flatfoot spacers, ideal for use on membranes
- Frost blankets
- Screed rails
- Screed chairs – plastic & metal
- Crack Inducers
- Tying Wire

Construction Accessories Ltd
Toughers Industrial Estate
Newhall, Naas,
Co. Kildare
Tel: 045-438691 Fax 045-438690
www.constructionaccessories.ie

Chapter 2 – OFFICE MANAGEMENT & RECORD KEEPING

Many Site Managers detest office work, and paperwork in general. The aim of this chapter is to identify the essential office tasks needed to run a site effectively, and to minimise the administrative work involved. There is no doubt that good record keeping is beneficial for all – including the Site Manager. There are some records which are pivotal to getting the job done successfully – and some which appear to have less relevance to the Site Manager.

Most forms of record floating around the site office can be categorised under one of three broad headings: - administration, communications and health and safety

Sometimes there is an overlap with documents falling under two, or maybe all three of theses headings. The Site Manager should keep the primary function of each document in mind when dealing with it. This is especially true when dealing with forms of communication.

Administrative records vary in importance greatly – but all exist for some purpose or other and the Site Manager will have to deal with them, or at least ensure that someone on the site deals with them.

2.1   The Site Diary

The site diary is probably the single most important document to be maintained on the site. If the Site Manager has delegated the filling of this to an engineer or site clerk, he should still examine it regularly, to ensure that it is maintained properly.

The following items should be recorded in the site diary:

- Daily weather conditions. A brief note on the prevalent weather conditions of the day should be recorded, This only needs one line, but is useful for making a claim later for delays caused by inclement conditions or settling disputes with sub-contractors over missed deadlines.

- Personnel on site. Personnel will be recorded in detail in the timesheets, but the total number of people on site should be recorded in the diary. This can be broken down by each subcontractor e.g. Carpenters x 5, Electricians x 6 etc. The list should also include all technical and management personnel.
- Visitors to the Site. The names of visitors to the site should be recorded.
- Results of all quality tests carried out should be noted.
- Works carried out that day. A reasonably detailed record should be made of progress made on that day. This should state the location of where the works took place and who carried out the work.
- Notes on Instructions received. Details of any instructions received from the architect engineer or directly from the client. Again this will be the subject of other record sheets but should be summarised in the diary with the reference number of any C.V.I. (See 2.17 below.)
- Note of any accidents or reportable incidents. These will be fully recorded in the Accident Book (see 2.24 below) but a brief note should be entered in the diary.
- Any other notable occurrences. If some unusual event occurred on the site it should also be recorded in the site diary.

2.2   Drawings

Drawings should be held together on a clip designed for the purpose, which is available from specialist stationary suppliers. The architect's drawings will deal with what the building or project will *look* like, while the consulting engineers drawings will show the *structural* details.

All drawings should be date stamped the minute they are received. If a date stamper is not available, then the date received should be clearly written in ink on the drawing, along with the name of the recipient. Sometimes revised drawings will be received after the work, which is the subject of the revision, has been commenced or completed. The Site Manager should resist the impulse to verbally attack or abuse the architect or engineer for supplying a "late detail" irrespective of how tempting it might be to do so. Instead, the Site Manager should record the time the revised drawing was received and should sent a memo to head office immediately, notifying them of the late detail and the amount of work to be changed. He should seek direction from head office before progressing. Sometimes the alteration may not be viable due to cost or time implications.

2.3   Drawing Register

The architect and the consulting engineers will normally supply a drawing register with all drawings issued. If this register is not immediately available the Site Manager should compile his own. This register should note the following:

- Drawing **number**,
- **Revision indicator** of the drawing, (e.g. Revision A, B, C etc.)
- The **date** the drawing was **issued,**
- The **title** of the drawing.

Architects and Engineers drawings should be clipped separately and separate registers maintained. Superseded drawings should be removed from the clip the minute a revision is received and the superseded drawings should be stamped 'Superseded' and stored safely on the site.

Occasionally an architect or engineer will issue a specific detail for some part of the works that was unclear, or omitted, from the earlier drawings. This detail should be recorded in the drawing register also, even if it doesn't have a reference number or other identification supplied by the architect or engineer.

2.4   Superseded Drawings

Superseded drawings are drawings that have been amended or updated or otherwise changed. Superseded drawings are very important documents for backing up a claim for additional payments or variations and as such should be stamped as '*Superseded*' the minute the revision is received, and the date of the revision should be noted on the superseded drawing. Superseded drawings should be stored carefully out of sight in the office to prevent confusion with current drawings. The chances are that a superseded drawing left lying round in clear view will be used by someone - irrespective of how clearly the word *superseded* appears. There's a danger that the very detail that has changed will be the first to be carried out. The contractor will never get paid for work carried out to a superseded drawing if he has received the revision on time and ignored the alterations. The superseded drawing should remain on site as it may be needed to cross check something later, especially if some of the work was commenced before the altered drawing was received.

2. 5   Goods Received Report

Head office will require proof that the goods appearing on supplier's invoices were actually delivered to the site. A goods inward report is compiled on a regular basis on site, and the delivery documents received from suppliers for that period, (usually weekly,) are attached to the report and returned to head office. This report and the attached documents are then processed for payment.

The Site Manager should complete the goods inwards report himself. He should not delegate this task. By physically completing the goods inward report himself, he will be very well informed on deliveries and shortages. He will gain a mental picture of the entire materials situation; a much better image that he will get from reading reports, talking to the yardman, etc.

Some simple system should be in place for filing or storing goods received dockets once they arrive on site. This can be a plastic wallet, a box or an opened-out coat hanger. Anything can be used that will hold the dockets together, and stop them from flying about the office once a door is opened.

The first step in preparing goods inwards reports is to establish that the goods were actually received, were in good order, suitable for their purpose and that the supplier's delivery note is correct. A procedure should be in place whereby the yardman, signing the documents as the deliveries are received, carries out a physical count of the items and checks their suitability. Any problems should be reported to the Site Manager by way of notes written on the actual delivery docket received or some other form of written communication. <u>It is no use simply signing the docket without checking the delivery.</u>

Dockets for goods which are incorrect, unsuitable, damaged, or won't be used for whatever reason, should be kept apart form the other documents and should be dealt with separately.

Assuming all is correct the next step is to write up the actual report. This will normally take the form of a pre-printed book or sheets where the details can be entered. Some firms use computerised reporting, but while the medium will differ, the information required won't.

Prior to filling out the goods inwards report, the delivery dockets should be sorted into groups, categorised first by supplier and then by date; this will minimise the amount of writing involved. The name of the supplier need only be written-in once on each page of the goods inwards report, regardless of how many delivery dockets exist from that supplier. This is equally true with the date.

In a similar way all dockets with similar materials should be pre-sorted to minimise repetitive entries of common words.

For delivery documents received for incorrect goods as described earlier, these documents should be entered in a different report which, in addition to the information entered for the suitable goods, contains details of the shortage or unsuitability.

The Site Manager should set aside a particular time each week for this task, perhaps a particular afternoon, when there are no meetings scheduled and many of that day's "fires" are either under control or extinguished. He should not let himself be distracted from carrying out this task at this regular time. And <u>he should not leave the site that day until the task is completed.</u>

2.6   Measures & Valuations

These fall into two categories, valuations for head office to claim from the client, and valuations for subcontractors to claim from the main contractor. In other words – *money in* and *money out*.

The Quantity Surveyor or someone else from head office, may ask the Site Manager to make an assessment of the works done to date for the purposes of submitting an interim valuation to the client. The Site Manager should keep this assessment factual – to put it simply he should not exaggerate. Sometimes it may be tempting to report more progress than that actually carried out – the feel good factor and all that, but the reality is that this usually comes back to haunt the Site Manager. He should keep his report factual and let head office personnel exaggerate or understate as they wish. Indeed if anything, the Site Manager should understate progress. This gives him a bit of slack, and things won't look as bad as was expected if head office representatives drop in to the site unexpectedly.   Copies of the relevant sheets should be filed away out of sight. It might prove problematic if the architect strayed into the site office and found evidence which contradicted the claim submitted by head office.

In the case of Sub Contractors valuations, the Site Manager may again be asked to make an assessment of works done. The Site Manager should be fair in his assessment – again leave any trimming-back of the valuation to head office, if they so choose. The natural tendency in the industry, is not to pay the sub contractor right up to date – just in case he would disappear off the job, with the most profitable part of his work completed. This would leave the main contractor with the costly small items to complete and this scenario can be a nightmare to sort out. But even if he is not paid up to date, recognition should be given to total amount of work actually carried out by the sub-contractor.

The Site Manager should remember that he is the leader of the team on the site. If head office has a policy of withholding payments to sub-contractors it can be very beneficial to the Site Manager to be seen to be *'on the side of the sub-contractor'* so to speak, and not be implicated in the withholding tactics.   The withholding policy should be '*distanced*' from the site and the Site Manager. It's easier to work with people than against them, and the sub-contractor is likely to be more co-operative with a Site Manager who is helpful rather than difficult in the highly emotional issue of payments. Management of cash-flow is such an important – often the dominant - issue for sub-contractors, that the Site Manager should steer totally clear of involvement in the process if possible.

2.7   Plant & Equipment Register

The plant & equipment register is a list of all of the plant and equipment on the site and a note of its working time, standing time and down time. It is normally compiled weekly and is useful for the Site Manager to keep track of plant and equipment on the site. Its primary function is for head office to keep track of the p & e and control costs. The p & e register can be tedious and difficult to keep up to date. This is an office function that can be delegated to the yardman, but the Site Manager should crosscheck it regularly for accuracy.

2.8   Hire Register

It's inevitable somewhere throughout the job that something will be hired in. A tight means of controlling plant and equipment hired in to the site should be maintained. Some form of a notice board could be used in the site office to keep track of hired items, with their details including hired-in date, clearly visible to the Site Manager. The disadvantage of this is that head office representatives will see this notice board too when they visit, and may ask the Site Manager questions that he may not want to answer in relation to hire issues. A note pad or special diary for hire-only items could be used, and would certainly be more private, but would lack the stark reminder quality of the notice board.

Whatever method of recording hire items is used, it should be remembered that hire must be tightly controlled, as costs can escalate quickly and items can 'disappear' without a trace if proper controls aren't in place.

2.9 Photographic Records

Photographic records can be very useful for a number of purposes. They may serve as a record of how things were before work commenced or of work that will be covered up later, like foundations etc.

Technological advancements now mean that you can record images digitally onto a camera memory rather that on to conventional film. The digital images can be loaded on to a computer using a cable interconnecting the two. These images can be sent electronically worldwide over the telephone line by e-mail, almost instantly. This technology offers many advantages in terms of speed, and is great if you need to get a picture to an architect or consulting engineer quickly. Getting an equally quick response from the same architect or engineer may be a different story however.

Digital images can be printed off and viewed and stored in the same way conventional prints would.

All this technology is fine if the Site Manager is computer literate. If not, as is often the case, then technology will be of no benefit because he simply won't use it – unless of course he delegates the task.

Conventional film cameras are normally simple to use, and the film itself can be stored; or it can be developed, and the prints stored. The latter option is more costly but at least you know what you have or have not captured on the film.

It is important that the images are stored safely be it on the computer or in the filing cabinet. If the film is not developed a label should be attached to it clearly indicating the job or site reference, and some note should also be attached stating what works were recorded on the film and the date. Some cameras have a facility to imprint the date onto the film but as a habit I believe that the date should be noted on the label also.

If the prints are stored the date can be written on the back of them along with the job or site reference and any relevant details. If the images are captured digitally and are to be stored on the computer, they should be placed in an appropriately named folder and should be backed up on to a compact disc or other similar medium.

General photographic tips.

When taking photographs for record purposes the following points should be considered:

- Include some reference to size or perspective in the picture. This can be an everyday object like a shovel when recording excavations or low walls etc., or the staff or a tape measure to indicate size. Just remember to include something that will give an indication of the scale of the subject, when someone else is looking at the picture. The photograph may be used in court and may be viewed by people who never stood on a site.

- It is also necessary to include something in the picture which will identify the photograph as belonging to that site. Maybe an adjoining building or local landmark will help prove that the picture was indeed of what you claim it was.

- Try and take the picture when the sun is behind you but watch out for strong shadows which may obscure the very item which you were trying to show. Generally the sun should be at your shoulder, and you may have to take the picture at a different time as a result. Shooting into the sun is not recommended. Looking through the viewfinder directly into the sun might damage your eyesight, and the picture won't show much detail of your subject.

- Many point & shoot cameras have a setting which when pressed calculates the exposure required for the picture. This is normally the main operation button, and the readings are taken when the button is partially pressed. If you are taking a picture into a bright sky or background, there is a risk of under-exposure, as the camera will take much of its reading from the bright sky. It is a good idea to take a reading from a darker scene, and without releasing the button, re-compose the picture before the switch is the fully depressed. This way the camera "thinks" it is taking a picture of something darker, and the resultant image should be satisfactory.

2.10 Requisitions

The requisition is used to do just that - request materials or plant. It is issued by the site to head office and is dealt with by the purchasing department. See Chapter 6.

2.11 Specifications

The specifications is a document prepared by the architect or engineer, detailing the type of materials and working methods to be used in the job, the allowable tolerances for measurements and tests, and other "rules" setting out the requirements of storage of materials etc. Following the specifications should ensure that the project is completed to the required quality standard.

The specifications usually form part of the contract documents and should be read thoroughly by the Site Manager before work commences on the site. If the job has commenced before the Site Manager is appointed, he should read the specifications immediately on getting to site, and note any works that appear to be progressing in a manner inconsistent with the specifications. He should contact head office immediately and seek clarification as to the reason for the inconsistency. Perhaps there was agreement on site regarding the alteration, or perhaps the inconsistency is part of the reason why the post of Site Manager had become vacant.

The Site Manager should ensure that all works proceed according to the specifications. When a particular type of product is specified for use in the job, the Site Manager should ensure that this precise product is in fact used. If this product is not available or is outside the budget that the contractor has set for the item, the Site Manager should contact the design team proposing an available and affordable substitute. Written agreement should be sought for the change. The way that this is handled on site is very much dependant to the style of operation of the parties involved, the relationship between the design team on the one hand, and the Site Manager and the contractor on the other. The Site Manager should take care that any apparent savings made by substitution of materials, does not come back to haunt the contractor in the form of deduction, or reduction, in the price received later. In other words it is fine using a cheaper alternative so long as the contractor gets the original price for the work.

Before a substitution is offered to the client, architect or engineer, the Site Manager should inform head office and involve them early on in the process. The Site Manager should ensure that head office is happy with the proposed substitution.

2.12   Sub-Contracts

Sub Contracts are used to "sell-off" part of the main contract to specialists who are equipped and have expertise in the particular work. The management of sub contractors is a major issue for the Site Manager, and is dealt with in detail in Chapter 8. The sub-contract is in fact a contract in its own right and this is dealt with in Chapter 4.

2.13   Timesheets

Time sheets are part of the paper trail of labour management. They fall primarily into four categories:

Daily time sheets are primarily used for calculating wages, and as such should be treated with appropriate importance by the Site Manager. Great care should be taken to get the details right, especially in small and medium sized sites where there may not be a signing-in/out register in place.

The Site Manager must ensure that the daily timesheet is returned to head office on time as delays can result in wages not getting into the bank on time - which can have a knock on effect on productivity. If there's a problem with someone's wages, the last thing the Site Manager wants is for that problem to be of his own making. After all he is the leader of the team on the site. Mistakes in wages should originate at head office.

Some companies require **weekly time sheets** in addition to daily time sheets, and the Site Manager may be sceptical of their usefulness – given that he has already completed the daily sheet. These sheets are used by Quantity Surveyors to allocate costs against the job. Filing out these sheets is a task that the Site Manager can delegate, and check from time to time that they are kept up to date.

Agency labour timesheets are dual purpose – they are used to calculate the wages of the individuals involved and are also used to by the agency to charge the contractor for the labour. The Site Manager must take great care with timesheets for agency labour because of the cost implications for his employers.

The Site Manager should be aware of how the agency is charging for the labour. Most agencies charge a rate per hour, with a premium for overtime. Smaller or local agencies may charge a day rate. The Site Manager needs to know the exact terms on which the agency is engaged, so that he can utilise the agency labour to the maximum benefit. He needs to know what the arrangements are for lunch-breaks and inclement weather, and how these are to be treated on the page.

As with the daily timesheets, the sheets need to be returned to the agency on time – to ensure that the operatives are paid. It's most important to return a copy to head office immediately and not to let these sheets build-up unreturned.

The Site Manager should draw lines with his pen, through any unused lines on the timesheet, to minimise the risk of unscrupulous agency personnel adding-in any names to the sheet before it gets back to the head office.

The guidance above applies to labour hired in on a "dayworks" basis as well as directly from a labour agency.

Labour allocation sheets are used to record the activities of each worker on the site. Quantity surveyors theoretically read the labour allocation sheets for costing purposes. Labour allocation sheets are also useful to accurately estimate how long specific tasks take for future programming or tendering. In addition, the main contractor can use them as supporting documentation to a claim.

Labour allocation sheets are sometimes read by Contracts Managers, and the information ascertained then used to cross examine Site Managers on resource use and efficiency.

2.14   Memos

The Memo is a vital weapon in the Site Manager's arsenal. It can serve as a reminder, as official notification, or as a word of advice.

Memos should be numbered from 01 upwards for the specific job. They should be used for record purposes and can be strategically used to maximise the advantage of the writer.

When should a memo be used?   The Site Manager should use the memo to commit to paper, anything, which is to his distinct advantage to do so now or may be later, and should avoid creating memos likely to have the opposite effect.   The memo is a great weapon and should be treated with utmost respect.

When preparing a memo, the Site Manager should pay particular attention to the following:

- Keep in mind *who* will read it.
- What do you want to say in the memo?
- Is there anything you *don't* want to say?
- Keep it short and to the point.
- Write it out rough first, and read it over before you send it.
- Take care with the tone – does it sound like you want it to sound?
- Keep a copy.

The memo should be written in language appropriate to the situation.   Sometimes when people write – the tone of the correspondence is much colder that if the words were spoken. When the memo is written, the writer should read it over carefully, to ensure that it says what was intended. This might seem an obvious point, but some people loose direction when they start writing and the memo can end up saying something slightly or even totally different, to that what was originally intended.

Memos received should be filed carefully as they may form part of a later claim.

2.15   Faxes

With the ease of use, and document sending speed of fax machines, it's no wonder that they have become so popular as a medium of communication.

Most of the points raised in relation to the preparation of memos, above, are relevant for fax communications as well.

Faxes should be filed away after they are either sent or received. Received faxes should be date stamped and if relevant time stamped. Original received documents should be photocopied - only the copy should be in use and the original filed away.

2.16   E-Mail

Electronic mail is a relative new technological advancement and an excellent one at that. Essentially, documents are created on the computer and are sent usually via a telephone line to a computer somewhere else. Because of the paperless nature of e-mail, documents and messages can be almost "invisible," unless a copy is printed off. Another problem is speed. Because an e-mail can be created and sent in a very short time, there is a risk that things will be written in the heat of the moment, that might be written differently had a cooling off period elapsed. Perhaps the communication might not have been issued at all, had the author cooled off first. Because of this immediacy, e-mail can be both a fantastic tool and a dangerous one.

E-mail should be filed in the hard disk of the computer and a paper copy of important documents should be printed-off and filed in the site office.

2.17   Confirmation of Verbal Instruction (C.V.I.)

The C.V.I. is a written record of a verbal instruction received from the design team or the client. It is used to *confirm* the verbal instructions. The written confirmation removes the risk of people forgetting or attempting to deny what was said, at a later stage.

Denial has a habit of popping up when the final account is presented and/or the job is over budget or in danger of becoming so.

The Site Manager should confirm in writing, the following details:

- The name of the person issuing the instruction.
- The exact instruction received.
- The specific location to which the instruction refers.
- The date and time that the instruction was received.
- Any other relevant information.

This written confirmation should be presented to the architect or engineer as soon as possible after the instruction was received, and a copy should be issued immediately to head office and a copy should also be filed in the site office.

Some firms have pre-printed books for this purpose and others have a special form saved on computer. Irrespective of what style the firm uses, the written confirmation of instructions received should be treated as one of the most important documents the Site Manager will have to deal with. The C.V.I. will form much of the basis of claims for variations and or extras at final account stage.

What constitutes a verbal instruction is a matter of interpretation. If a particular instruction suits the Site Manager he should follow it up immediately with a C.V.I. If on the other hand, an instruction doesn't suit the Site Manager or head office, then he may be well advised to hold-off in the hope that the architect or engineer involved may issue a more favourable instruction later.

The Site Manager must always be conscious of the best interests of his employers when it comes to dealing with the client, the architect or the structural engineers. He must be alert at all times and should never rush to do something that suits either the client or his representatives, just because he is asked or told to do so. The request or instruction may have cost, time or resource implications for the contractor and these may not be recoverable from the client.

Verbal instructions therefore are to be accepted or subtly and discretely rejected as the Site Manager thinks fit, keeping in mind the best interests of his employers. After all as we said in Chapter 1 - it may well end up in court.

2.18   Request For Information (R.F.I.)

The R.F.I. is used to communicate, in written form, the need for more information. It is issued directly to the architect or the engineers unless there is a Clerk of Works or Resident Engineer on site. The R.F.I. can be used as part of a later claim for extra payment caused by insufficient information or by delays. As a result it should be used very carefully and strategically. There are a number of considerations to be kept in mind before the R.F.I. is issued:

- Are you certain that you don't have the information already? You'll look foolish if you ask for something you already have.
- Is it in your best interests to put it in writing at this stage? Perhaps a quiet word before the next site meeting or maybe a phone call might produce a better result. Architects and Engineers know that when they see something coming at them in writing it can have later consequences, and they may strike back in some way that doesn't suit the Site Manager.
- Following on from the above point, if you put the request in writing at this stage, will the reply suit your needs and that of the contractor? What are the potential replies to your query and do they all suit your needs? What if the reply is tactically totally unsuitable?

The R.F.I. is part of the politics of the job and should be treated strategically. The implications of an unfavourable response may be very significant, so the Site Manager should carefully consider (a) if the request should be put in writing at all, (b) if it should be put in writing now, and (c) what are the potential responses; which one suits best, and can the request be written in such a way as to get the most desirable response?

2.19   Accident Report

The first point to remember when compiling an accident report is that it is just that, a *report* <u>not</u> an accident *investigation.*

The Site Manager should take great care when compiling an accident report. He can only record what he witnessed. If he did not witness the accident his report should be based on what is told to him, not what he suspects happened. And he should be extremely careful to keep his report factually accurate. It is very easy in the excitement of the moment to make presumptions or to omit some important piece of information.

Where the Site Manager <u>did not witness the accident himself</u>, the report should include:

- The name of the victim and the name of his employer.
- The name of the person who reported the accident.
- The date and time that the accident was reported.
- The names of any witnesses and the names of their employers.
- A brief statement of the events as they took place along the following lines:

    o At 10.30 am on Wednesday July 7th 20** James Kelly an employee of ABC Carpentry, notified me that his colleague Michael Hunt had fallen from a scaffold at the rear of House no 6. Mr Kelly said the accident happened five minutes previously. Accompanied by Mr. Kelly, I went to the area in which the alleged accident took place and found Mr. Hunt lying on the ground, apparently in some discomfort. He was conscious and there were no visible injuries – no cuts bruises or bleeding. I immediately rang for an ambulance. I instructed Mr Kelly to get a blanket from my vehicle in the car park and this was used to cover Mr. Hunt. I remained at the scene with Mr Kelly until the ambulance arrived at 10.55am. The leader of the ambulance crew [insert his/her name] then took charge and Mr Hunt was removed from the site at 11.10am. by ambulance to the local hospital. I checked the scaffolding from where Mr. Kelly allegedly fell; it seemed in order and work recommenced on the site at 11.20 am.

• What action the Site Manager took.

If the Site Manager actually witnessed the accident, his report will be very similar, but will include an accurate description of what he saw. There is no place in an accident report for words like could and should.

The accident report should be sent to head office and should not be shown or given to anyone else. From this point on the accident is exclusively a head office matter and the Site Manager should refrain from discussing it with anyone other than his superiors at head office.

2.20 Fás Safe Pass Register

A register of the details of the Fás Safe Pass Certificate of every worker on the site should be maintained. Workers not in possession of these cards should not be permitted to work on the site. This is a simple document to prepare and will be very useful to present to any HSA representative that may visit the site. A sample of a typical Safe Pass Register is attached in Schedule1 at the rear of this book.

2.21 Filing System.

One of the first tasks facing the Site Manager when a new project commences is the establishment of a decent filing system on the site. On small to medium sized sites, a locking four-drawer steel filing cabinet is an absolute necessity. The Site Manager must resist attempts to use the cabinet for storage of instruments, first aid materials, p.p.e., teabags etc. If cabinet space is required for these items, a second cabinet should be sourced, but the filing cabinet should not be used for any purpose other than *filing of records and documents.*

That said, the Site Manager needs to clearly define what goes where and should communicate this decision to anyone who will use the cabinet. In addition, he could label each drawer clearly with large adhesive labels.

One of the drawers in the cabinet should be dedicated to correspondence to and from head office, the design team and the client. Another drawer should be dedicated to documentation from suppliers. A third drawer should hold all the documentation relative to sub-contractors. This leaves the fourth drawer divided between health & safety documentation and quality control.

On some sites a single cabinet may be needed for each of the items listed above − and as a result, several filing cabinets may be needed. The critical point is to have a dedicated, lockable place for each type of document, make sure that it is filed where it should be filed to aid rapid retrieval, and don't let other items infiltrate the space. The filing system has to be designed in a way that is practical, and it has to be maintained. The Site Manager must intervene at the first sight of misuse of the filing cabinet; physically removing the offending items if necessary, and must police the system firmly.

Hanging, or suspension, files should be used in each drawer, with the card clearly completed in block capitals and then inserted in the plastic tab which should carefully be clipped into the top of the file. This sounds like such a basic detail as to be unworthy of print space, but its importance cannot be sufficiently stressed.

A separate file should be maintained for each supplier and subcontractor. A separate file should be maintained for each type of document in the other drawers. These would include daily timesheets, weekly timesheets, p & e registers, concrete cube registers, cube reports, etc. A place for everything, and − everything in its place. It is a cliché, but as a system it works and it's the Site Manager's responsibility to ensure it does.

2.22   Product/ Materials Data Sheets

Product data sheets state the storage, handling and application details for the specific product to which they refer. Both manufacturers and suppliers issue these sheets, and after all concerned on the site has read them, they should be filed. These sheets can be built up by the Site Manager over time and should be brought from one site to the next as the materials used won't change all that much.

2.23   Issue of P.P.E.

When personal protective equipment (p.p.e.) has been issued the recipient should sign a sheet, confirming his acceptance of the p.p.e.. There are a number of reasons for this.

- It helps prevent accidents.
- The operative can't use an excuse that he doesn't have, or didn't get, the particular item of p.p.e.
- It serves a means of controlling the actual equipment.
- It will demonstrate that you are taking p.p.e. and health and safety issues seriously when head office representatives or HSA personnel call to the site.
- The item may be contra-chargeable to a sub-contractor on the site.

The Site Manager should ensure that a copy of the Issue of P.P.E. Register is sent to head office weekly.

2.24   Accident Book

Accidents on the site should be recorded in the Accident Book. The book should be available for inspection in the site office. At the end of the job all accident books should be returned to head office and a new book should be used for each site or project. In the past it was possible to buy pre-printed accident books, but they seem to have disappeared from the market. If he can't find one, a hard-cover copy should be used – one that is sturdy and in which the pages are well bound.

2.25   Safety Statements

The main contractor should provide a safety statement for each new project and this should be available in the site office for inspection.

The Site Manager should not allow any sub contractor to commence work on site unless he has submitted a copy of his safety statement to the site. Copies sent to head office are unacceptable for site purposes – the statement must be on the site at all times where the sub-contractor is working. The safety statement should reflect the current regulations, and should be signed by the managing director. Works on the site should progress in accordance with the procedures set out in the safety statement.

2.26   Risk Assessments

A risk assessment is just that – an assessment of risk. Risk assessments have a logical place in the hierarchy of health and safety. Unless risks are identified and assessed, it's going to be difficult to protect people from them. Many subcontractors deal with risk assessments in a haphazard way. In some cases the sub contractor will present a safety statement which has a section dealing with risks associated with his work. How can he possibly give an accurate assessment of risk for a particular site, in such a remote manner? The Site Manager must adopt a firm position in the area of risk assessment, and if necessary sit down with the sub contractor and help prepare the assessment. (See Chapter 10)

2.27   Method Statements

Method statements follow on from, or are a response-to, risk assessments. These statements describe how are particular task is to be carried-out, after the assessment of the risk has been examined. (See Chapter 10)

The method statements should be filed safely in the site office, and, needless to say, the work should be carried-out in accordance with the method statement. After all it is a *method statement!*

2.28   CR Forms -Construction Regulation Forms

CR Forms are required under current regulation and the relevant forms should be filed in the site office. For the complete list of CR forms, see Schedule 6 at the rear of this book.

2.29   Safe System Of Work Plan (SSWP)

Different types of SSWP are in operation for different tasks on site. These include ground works, house building, demolition, civil engineering and new commercial building construction. The forms are issued by the Health & Safety Authority, and are absolutely excellent in their comprehensiveness and simplicity. The forms use simple easy to understand drawings, and are available in several languages. The Site Manager should insist in their use and that all workers involved sign the form.

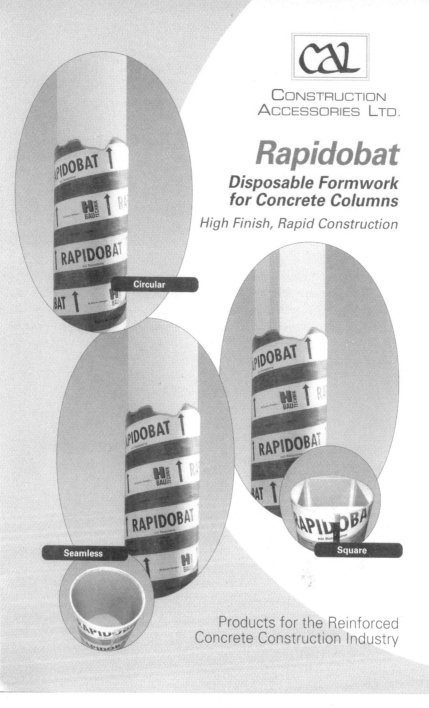

CONSTRUCTION
ACCESSORIES LTD.

Rapidobat

**Disposable Formwork
for Concrete Columns**

High Finish, Rapid Construction

Circular

Seamless

Square

Products for the Reinforced
Concrete Construction Industry

Chapter 3 – MEETINGS

3.1   Surviving The Meetings.

Meetings seem to occur with greater frequency in our lives now than ever before. When you ring an office asking to speak with someone chances are you'll be told, "He's in a meeting." On site, there are site meetings, sub-contractor meetings, safety meetings etc.

So how does the Site Manager survive all these meetings and can he turn them to his advantage?

The Site Manager should note the following points for all meetings:

- Anticipate and be prepared.
  - o What's likely to come-up and how can it be fielded?
  - o The Site Manager should never go into a meeting "cold."
- Plan carefully.
  - o The Site Manager should plan his tactics carefully in advance of the meeting – it's dangerous practice to "make it up as you go along."
- Look out for non-verbal communication.
  - o Not all communication at meetings is verbal. Look out for facial expressions, body language and any other signals you can pick up.
- Under promise and over achieve.
  - o Don't promise more than is absolutely necessary – people have a nasty habit of remembering broken promises.
  - o It is much better to achieve more, rather than less, than was promised.
- Resist temptation to "have a go" at someone at the meeting despite the opportunities which may present.
  - o You will nearly always get a better opportunity later.

     o   Keep your powder dry. The Site Manager must remain cool and calm at meetings.
- Start and finish with positives.
     o   Starting with positives relaxes the other people at the meeting and can defuse tricky situations.
     o   Finishing off with positives leaves a more pleasant aftertaste.

3.2 Types Of Meetings

Meetings take many forms, take place in many locations and serve many different purposes. Indeed the one meeting can serve different purposes for the parties in attendance.

The Site Manager will more than likely have to attend or arrange the following types of meetings during the course of his working day:

- The Site Meeting – Client & Design Team
- Meetings on site with the Clerk of Works
- The Site Meeting – Reporting Progress To Head Office
- Sub Contractor Meetings
- Safety Meetings
- Strategy Meetings
- Meetings With Suppliers
- Disciplinary Meetings

3.2.1 The Site Meeting – Client & Design Team.

This meeting will be held at regular intervals, maybe weekly or fortnightly, on the site. The attendance will include the design team – the architect and the design engineers, usually the client, and representatives of head office. As the job progresses nominated sub-contractors may also be in attendance – especially for part of the meeting at least.

At this meeting progress will be reported, problems will be discussed – some will be solved – others simply deferred. Documentation is regularly exchanged at these meetings – requests for information from the contractor, new or revised drawings issued by the designers.

The Site Manager should have his wits about him at these meetings as he can be quizzed intensely at one meeting when he may least expect it, and not even be looked-at, at another when he is fully prepared. The meeting is usually preceded by a "walk-about" where all the visitors have a look at how the job is progressing since the last meeting.

3.2.2   Meetings with the Clerk of Works

Many sites have a resident Clerk of Works or a Resident Engineer, supervising the works on behalf of the client. The Site Manager will have numerous meetings and encounters with either or both. If everything is going well on the site, for all parties, these meetings will usually be friendly. Sometimes however, the relationship between the contractor's representatives and the Clerk of Works or Resident Engineer can be strained, with a coldness and distrust between the parties. The facts of life for the Site Manager are very simple – he must work with these people on a daily basis, so he has to make the best of it.

Formal meetings between the two should be minuted, and the minutes circulated to both parties as well as head office. The Site Manager should be fully prepared for the meeting and be tactically alert.

The Site Manager should make every effort to cooperate with the client's representatives on site and strive for a harmonious relationship. He should approach the working association on the basis that both sides have a job to do, and where significant difference of opinion exists, could try some tactic to defuse any tension as soon as it starts to build up. He could, for example, tell the Clerk of Works or Resident Engineer that he agrees with their proposals personally, but that he is under pressure from head office to do things differently. He could try to establish empathy for his situation, and ask advice on how he could get around the problem. Frequently the Clerk of Works or Resident Engineer might offer a compromise proposal, which would be mutually acceptable. In this case the Site Manager should thank his counterpart for his help.

3.2.3   The Site Meeting – Reporting Progress To Head Office

This meeting may immediately precede or follow the Client & Design Team Meeting. This is where the Site Manager gives an account of how the job is progressing to the representatives from head office, which may include Contracts Manager, Quantity Surveyor and Director in charge of the project.

The Site Manager will often be expected to present a Progress Report (discussed in Chapter 5) at the meeting and a revised and/or a marked-up programme. Existing or potential problems will be discussed and, depending on the style of the firm, the Site Manager may be "interrogated" at the meeting. While some Site Managers find this stressful, it should be remembered that this, in reality, might be the only opportunity that head office has, to find out the true position on site. The "interrogation" of the Site Manager, may not be viewed in that way at all by head office. It may seem to them, simply as a routine examination of the up-to-date state of the job. Site Managers are however, normally delighted when the head office personnel get into their cars and leave him to get on with the job.

The Site Manager should thoroughly follow up on points raised by his superiors. These items may appear of little importance to the overall job, but it is likely that these are the things that will be focused on in the days immediately after the meeting, or at the next one.

3.2.4   Sub Contractor Meetings

These meetings should be held weekly, and all sub-contractors on the site should be included in the meeting. Since sub-contractors are normally "on a price" they won't want to spend long, so, like all meetings, it should be kept short and to the point.

At this meeting any difficulties between sub-contractors on the site should be ironed out, and progress should be appraised with a view to minimising the chances of one sub-contractor delaying another. While this is an ideal opportunity for the Site Manager to reprimand one sub-contractor for, say, poor workmanship, I believe that this should be avoided at the main weekly sub-contractor meeting. The offender should be called in for a separate meeting, where specifics about his workmanship can be handled without embarrassing the sub-contractor in full view of all of the other sub-contractors on the site.

Delays caused by a particular sub-contractor should be addressed at the meeting, and how the Site Manager deals with one sub-contractor will lay down a marker for the others.

The Site Manager should listen to each sub-contractor at the meeting and should be on the look out for non-verbal communication.

3.2.5   Safety Meetings

Safety Meetings should be held regularly on site and may consist of a meeting where all the workers on the site attend or if that is not practical, then the workforce should be broken into groups.

The purpose of the meeting should be to examine safety performance since the last meeting and to plan for the next stage of the job. Because of the developing nature of all construction projects, new risks may arise, and a safety meeting is a good place to highlight these new dangers.

Tool Box talks (discussed in Chapter 10) it should be noted, are not actually safety meetings – they are brief safety presentations.

The Site Manager should ensure that the meeting doesn't digress from the specific purpose for which it is called – safety issues. Minutes should be prepared when the meeting is completed, noting the topics covered and the points raised. As with all minutes, record should be made of those responsible for carrying out the various tasks, and these should be circulated to those present and copied to head office as soon as possible afterwards.

The Site Manager should ensure that an attendance register is signed by all present, and this should be filed in the site office.

3.2.6 Strategy Meetings

The Site Manager should hold Strategy meetings with his key on-site personnel, as necessary. The purpose of these meetings may be:

- To plan work,
- Share views on productivity and individual performance of sub-contractors,
- Discuss any problems that have arisen,
- Review the Health & Safety practices on site,
- Other general items specific to the job.

These meetings are often informal, and may be held over breakfast or at some other point in the day. The Site Manager should be prepared for them and have a written agenda –even if it just scribbled down quickly on a notepad. These meetings are essentially internal communication or briefing meetings.

The Site Manager should use the Strategy Meeting to issue instructions to other members of the site management team and key personnel. It can also be useful if he is updated on any events which occurred previously, unknown to him, or some other similar type of issue. The meetings frequently take the form of a general chat without the parties involved even being aware that the meeting is happening! The key issue for the Site Manager is to ensure that all interested parties are informed of instructions and the general policy to be followed on site. There is no absolute need for formal minutes, but the Site Manager should make a record of what happened and tasks allocated.

3.2.7 Meetings With Suppliers

Meetings with suppliers or their representatives are frequently unstructured, but the Site Manager should formalise meetings where critical delivery arrangements are made. Regular formal meetings with suppliers are essential if the supplier is responsible for some element of design, or for certain long lead items. As with sub-contractor meetings the minutes should be circulated to all present and all other interested parties as soon as possible after the meeting.

3.3   Agenda

The agenda is the list of business to be conducted at the meeting. Agendas are very useful because they list the items or business of the meeting – minimising the risk of forgetting something important. They also can, if followed, prevent the discussion from wandering off the point and wasting time.

The architect will probably set the agenda for site meetings, and the Site Manager may have limited control over the structure or content of these meetings. The Site Manager will set the agenda for many of the other meetings and he will have full control of what appears on the list.

So what should appear on the list and what should be omitted? While this depends greatly on the type and purpose of the meeting and on the style of the Site Manager, he should generally keep the list as short as possible, and may include the following:

- Review of the minutes of the last meeting with follow-up action
- Specific and clearly defined items for discussion at this meeting

The meeting should not wander away into areas of discussion that are irrelevant. The Site Manager, in his role as chair of the meeting, should ensure that everyone present has an opportunity to air his views, and that an opportunity is provided for questions to be dealt with.

3.4   Minutes

Minutes are a record of decisions taken at meetings and may have legal implications. These minutes may be used as the basis for a later claim for additional or varied payments from the original agreement. As such, great care should be exercised when compiling minutes.

The names of those attending, and a record of the items discussed and decisions taken at the meeting, should be recorded in the minutes. The names of those responsible for carrying out the various tasks or following up on them, should also be recorded.

This gives the writer a great opportunity to record events in a particular way, and the Site Manager should not shy away from compiling the minutes, given the chance. While no fabrication should be included, or no omissions made, the author of the minutes can give emphasis to a particular point debated, or give a general "complexion" to the entire document. In politics this is known as putting a "spin" on things!

In the case of Sub Contractor meetings, Safety meetings and Strategy meetings, the Site Manager will be expected to compile the minutes. The simplest method of doing this is to have sheets of notepaper pre-prepared, with a heading for each item on the agenda, and a number of lines available for writing-in, in longhand, decisions taken at the meeting or points raised. A column to the right of the page can be used to record the names of the person who is responsible for carrying out each particular task. (See sample – Schedule 2 at the rear of this book.)

These sheets can then be sent to the head office for typing, or can be read into a Dictaphone, and the tape sent to the office for typing. Alternatively if he has the time and is comfortable with typewriters or word processors, the Site Manager can type the minutes up himself.

Once typed-up and thoroughly checked for errors, the minutes should be circulated to those present at the meeting, and copy sent to head office. As with all documentation originating from or passing through the site, a copy should be filed in the site office.

3.5   Tactics For Meetings

The approach taken to any meeting can be very significant, and planning of tactics can be very beneficial. The seating arrangements at the meeting for example can be significant. The Site Manager may wish to prevent the Clerk of Works watching through the window, ongoing work on the site during the meeting. and as a result may choose to sit facing the window himself.

If he wishes the meeting to end quickly he may arrange for some works to be carried out near the meeting room, works that happen to be quite noisy, for example. Or he may "arrange" for the meeting to be disturbed by callers.

Whatever tactics he uses, the Site Manager may strategically gain an advantage by careful plotting events to coincide with the meeting, or disrupt it in some way. However, he must be very selective on what "arrangements" he makes, and whom he chooses as his co-conspirators, as any cheap tricks or any suspicions aroused, may backfire on him – leaving him embarrassed, with his credibility seriously damaged.

Products for Architectural Concrete

Stockists of the Pieri range of products for architectural finishes for concrete:

- Formliners
- Retarders for exposed aggregate
- Specialist release agents
- Concrete sealers

Finished surface having used a Pieri formliner.

Standard patterns available or designed to order.

Complete the architectural look to your surrounding grounds:
We supply concrete imprinting mats and colour dyes.

Also available is a complete range of patio slab moulds and mix-through colour dye to suit.

Construction Accessories Ltd
Toughers Industrial Estate
Newhall, Naas,
Co. Kildare
Tel: 045-438691 Fax 045-438690
www.constructionaccessories.ie

Chapter 4 – TERMS & DEFINITIONS

Disclaimer!

The list of terms set out in this chapter and the definitions attached to them is very limited. The purpose of the list is to identify terms that the Site Manager may come across – not from a construction point of view, but from interaction with clients, architects, design engineers, and head office personnel. The definitions are deliberately simplistic and cannot be taken as legal interpretations in any way. They are intended as a guide only.

Acceleration

Acceleration is a process whereby works on the site have to be speeded up to complete the project on time or ahead of schedule. This might involve working longer hours or double shifts, or perhaps at the weekend. The reason for the delay usually has nothing to do with contractor, and he normally gets paid accordingly.

Architect

The architect designs the building and provides the drawings and construction details to the builder. The client usually employs the architect, and he represents the client at site meetings and at other times.

Bench Marks

Reference points on the site, the level of which is known.

Bill Of Quantities (BQ)

The BQ is a description and quantity of each specific item, that the Surveyor can think of, before the job is given out for pricing. Tendering contractors apply rates to each item, and this forms the tender price. No Site Manager should ever rely on the accuracy of a BQ, as by their nature jobs and processes change, and Quantity Surveyors frequently over measure certain items at the preparation stage, to cover (in the tender sum) for any accidental omissions. This process is called over-measuring.

Bill Rates

The rates applied to the items listed in the Bill of Quantities at the time of tender.

Budget

The budget is the amount of money which head office is prepared to spend on each specific item (including plant, materials and labour) in the job. The budget amount has to be well under the amount tendered for each item, to provide for profit and to recover any losses incurred on any other item that may have gone over-budget.

Calibration

Calibration deals with checking the accuracy of specific instruments like, levels, Total Stations, etc. Accredited testing centres issue the certificates, and these should be sought by the Site Manager, should be checked, and copies should be filed on site. Notes should be made in the diary of expiry dates of the certificates.

Clerk of Works

The Clerk of Works is appointed by the client and is normally resident on the site. His job is to supervise all works and report to the architect or client. The Site Manager will have to work closely with the Clerk of Works, advising him of when certain works are due to take place, and providing the Clerk with an opportunity to check anything which is due to be covered-up. The Site Manager shouldn't forget that it is he, and not the Clerk of Works that's running the job, and not allow too many delays.

Contract

A contract is an agreement, giving rise to obligations enforced or recognised by law. A contract exists when legally capable persons have reached agreement, or where the law considers them to have reached agreement.
It confers rights to, and imposes obligations on each party.

Essentials Of A Contract:

- An Agreement
  - There must be agreement between the parties
- Intention To Be Contractually Bound
  - There must be intention
- Consideration
  - Consideration is payment of some kind
- Legally Capable Persons
  - What or who is a legally capable person? Basically everyone except:

    - A Minor
    - A Lunatic
    - A Drunk

A contract doesn't have to be in writing, but written ones are usually easier to enforce than verbal ones.

Critical Path

The critical path is a term used to describe the interaction between certain tasks on a programme. This usually refers to work which if incomplete would prevent the carrying out of other work. If the foundations aren't completed the walls can't be completed – therefore the construction of foundations would be on the critical path, until of course they were completed.

Datum

A level used from which all other levels on the site are calculated. The datum must be a point or surface which won't be disturbed during the construction process.

Dayworks

Dayworks are works which can't or won't be charged for on an otherwise measured basis.

Daywork Sheets

Daywork sheets should include the names and the trade of all operators involved, should list all plant and materials involved as well as any supplementary charges.

Drawing Register

The drawing register is a list containing, drawing names, numbers, revision numbers, and the date each drawing was issued. The circulation list should be also included in the register. Separate registers should be maintained for architects and engineer's drawings. The register should be on display in the office.

Drawing

Documents which detail what has to be built and where.

Engineer

An engineer is a person trained in engineering. The Site Manager will probably have to deal with Site Engineers (engaged by the main contractor) and Consulting Engineers (engaged by the client.) The Site Engineer is usually responsible for setting-out, checking levels and generally ensuring that the building is built in accordance with the drawings. The Consulting Engineers, sometimes known as Design Engineers are responsible for the provision of drawings and details. Resident Engineers are engaged by the client to supervise works in addition to a Clerk of Works on certain contracts.

Extension of Time

If the contract period overruns, the contractor may be entitled to payment in excess of the contract sum because he has to remain on the site longer than was originally envisaged. If the delays are the contractor's fault he won't get any extra money, but if the delays can be proven not to be his fault, he may get additional money through a process know as Extension of Time. This shouldn't be confused with extra work – which is normally chargeable at Bill Rates, new rates or dayworks.

Final Account

The final account is the final claim for payment by a sub-contractor or main contractor on a specific contract. It is a valuation of all works carried out, and a list of all payments received.

Front Loading

Is a term used to describe the drawing down of excessive sums of money early on in the contract. Demolitions or excavations are typical examples of tasks, which would be used to front load a payment schedule.

Grid Lines

Two sets of lines on the drawings, which are used as a setting-out and reference aid. The lines run at intervals, and one set runs at ninety degrees to the other.

Interim Valuations

Claims for payment made by sub-contractors or main contractors, based on works carried out, at intervals before the completion of the contact.

Liquidated Damages

If a contractor fails to complete a project by a certain date, pre-agreed at contract stage, he may be liable for liquidated damages. This is a pre-agreed sum of money deducted from the contract price, usually per week or month of overrun. Liquidated damages clauses are common in contracts within the industry, but the money is rarely deducted.

Long Lead Items

Long lead items is a term given to certain materials which not readily available. This would include any items that may have to be manufactured or imported, especially for the job. Examples include, windows, lift cars, etc.

Man Hours

A means of quantifying time and cost calculated by multiplying the number of hours worked, by the number of personnel involved. A job may take, say, four men six hours to complete – therefore it would be said to take twenty-four man-hours to complete.

Mobilisation
The process of moving on to the site.

Prime Cost Sums
This is a sum provided for work or materials to be supplied by a nominated sub-contractor or supplier. Examples might include plumbing, electrical, windows, finishes etc.

Programme
A project management tool drawn up to predict the commencement and completion dates of a project and each element of the works. Programmes are dealt with in Chapter 5

Progress Report
Report of progress made on each item on the programme.

Provisional Sum
A sum provided for costs which can not be clearly defined at the time of tender.

Retention
Amount of money held back on a contractor or sub contractor to ensure completion of works or defects. Usually calculated as a percentage of payment due or total payment.

Specifications
The specifications state how the job is to be built, and describes the materials and workmanship standards, the acceptable tolerances and testing required.. The specifications are issued by client and are drafted by the consulting engineers.

Sub-Structure
That part of the building below ground level.

Super Structure
That part of the building above ground level.

Superseded Drawings

Drawings which have been replaced with updated versions.

Tenders

Quotation presented for acceptance.

Unforeseen Conditions

Physical conditions or obstructions which could not have been reasonably foreseen by an experienced contractor.
Weather, or conditions cause by weather conditions are not included.

Formwork Accessories

For all your formwork requirements, Construction Accessories stock a full range of tiebar, wingnuts, waler plates as well as permanent formwork.

Perm-e-form is a rigid corrugated Polypropylene sheet used for ground Beams and pile caps. Perm-e-form is left in the ground after use affording contractors savings in time, labour and money.

Hy-Rib expanded metal is used for construction joints where scabbling would normally be required but needs to be avoided. Hyrib prevents injury from use of vibration tools and saves time.

Construction Accessories Ltd
Toughers Industrial Estate
Newhall, Naas, Co. Kildare
Tel: 045-438691 Fax 045-438690
www.constructionaccessories.ie

Chapter 5 – PROJECT MANAGEMENT
PROGRAMMING & PROGRESS REPORTS

5.1 The Programme

Almost every construction project uses a programme of some sort. While some Site Managers feel intimidated by them, and others simply ignore the programme, the reality is that if it is prepared realistically it is a very useful tool. Note the word *realistically* – well that's the key. If the programme is not realistic in its allocation of time for each task, it won't be used and its author will be the subject of jokes and ridicule.

A programme plots tasks against time. Most programmes are computer generated nowadays. Common types of programmes include the Gantt Chart, the Calendar and the Network Diagram. But the programme can still be drawn out on a sheet of paper and many Site Managers and Contracts Managers prepare the initial drafts of their programmes in this way.

5.1.1 The Gantt Chart

This is the most common type of programme used in the construction industry. It lists tasks down the left hand side of the page and time in units of days, weeks or months across the top. Horizontal bars are drawn to represent the length of time each task will take.

5.1.2 The Calendar View.

This presents the information in a weekly format overlaid on a calendar. It can be viewed by week, month or year.

5.1.3 The Network Diagram.

This is essentially a block diagram of tasks and their dependencies presented in flowchart form.

5.1.4   Methods of Preparation.

While there are many ways to present and view programmes, ultimately they are all the same in that someone has to list the tasks to be included in the programme and some method of providing for the time each task will take must be included.

The method whereby someone predicts or estimates how long each task will take to complete, is known as the *task driven* method of programme preparation.

The *time driven* method of preparation is based around the earliest start-date and required completion dates of the project, and lets the programme dictate how much time can be allocated to each task.

Most programmes are prepared using a combination of these two methods.

5.1.5   Task Descriptions & Different Types of Programmes.

Tasks may vary considerably in description depending on the level of detail required in the programme. In say a housing project, the task could be listed by the phases of the works. This type of programme would be totally impractical for construction purposes but may be helpful to the finance department for cash flow projections.

Similarly, a detailed programme broken down day by day into the various jobs to be undertaken in each house, would be great for construction, but would be far too detailed for cash flow management.

So straight away we see that there are different types of programmes required for the same job by different people, at the same time. Sounds confusing - doesn't it?   Well it gets even more confusing! Some firms have different programmes for the client and for internal-use; indeed most firms operate this way!

The responsibility for the production of the programme usually falls to the Contracts Manager, but the Site Manager should be able to produce a programme himself.

5.1.6 Duration

The duration of a task is initially estimated - someone guesses how long it will take to complete. This estimate is then entered into the programme. Later on, as the job progresses, it will be possible to complete an *actual* duration.

5.1.7 Linking Tasks

Linked tasks on a programme are tasks that are in some way connected. The second task can't be completed until the first one is either commenced or completed, for example foundations have to be excavated before the concrete and reinforcement can be placed into them. Equally the roof timbers need to be in place before the slating or tiling can be completed. These tasks are said to be linked. Examples of tasks with no connection or link would include electrical works inside a house and, say, the slating of the roof.

When preparing a programme, links have to be inserted to ensure that there is no conflict between connected tasks. But what happens when tasks don't need to be completed, only commenced, before the follow-on task can be commenced. Going back to the foundations example, excavation of one area could be completed, but the entire excavations needn't be completed, before reinforcement could be placed and concrete poured. In fact, pre-fabrication of the reinforcement could commence before the excavations were opened. This is where lead and lag times come into the programming.

5.1.8 Lag and Lead Times

A *lag time* is a delay between one task finishing and another task beginning. Concrete poured in the foundations will need some time to cure, before it can be loaded with walls etc. The specifications for the job may state that say, seven days are allowed to elapse before the walls can be commenced. This is a lag time of seven days.

For programming purposes a *lead-time* is an overlap between the tasks. Say it is estimated that excavation of the foundations will take five days, but that reinforcement-placing and concrete pouring could *commence* after two days. This produces a lead-time between the excavations and the other works, of three days.

5.1.9   The Critical Path

Every programme has a critical path. Items on the critical path can dictate progress and greatly impact the completion date. If any of the tasks on the critical path are delayed then the project itself will be delayed unless some form of intervention takes place to make up the lost time – if this is possible.

To illustrate a simple project – that of the construction of a single house, the tasks included in a programme might include the following items:

1.   Mobilise
2.   Strip Site
3.   Excavate Foundations
4.   Pour Foundations
5.   Ground Floor Slab
6.   Erect Timber Frame
7.   Felt & Batten Roof
8.   Sheet Roof
9.   Fit Windows & External Doors
10. External Masonry
11. First Fix Mechanical
12. First Fix Electrical
13. First Fix Carpentry
14. Insulate & Board
15. Tape & Fill Joints or Skim
16. Second Fix Mechanical
17. Second Fix Electrical
18. Second Fix Carpentry
19. Decorate
20. External Render
21. Drives & Landscape
22. Snag
23. Demobilise

One of the advantages of timber-frame housing is that once the frame is erected, the windows and doors are in, and the roof is felted, all inside works can proceed. The project is no longer weather dependant. The pace at which the external works proceed is not as important as in traditional build methods.

The first and most obvious item on the critical path is to get the foundations completed for delivery and erection of the timber frame. As the date for delivery of the frame will have been agreed in advance with the factory supplying the frame, this date becomes a *milestone* on the programme. The foundations will have to be completed before the frame can be erected.

The next key aspect of the programme will be the weathering of the building so that internal finishing can commence. Here, the installation of windows and external doors and the sheeting of the roof are key factors.

Once the building is weathered, the pace and sequence of internal works can be adjusted, if practical, without any knock on effect on the handover date. The external works can proceed at a slower pace than normal, again with no handover implications.

The critical path is easy to see in the example above. Items on the critical path cease to be on the critical path once completed.

5.1.10 Advantages of a realistic programme.

There are many advantages to be gained from a realistic programme. The financial controller will be able to forecast cash flow and make whatever arrangements are necessary. Purchasing will know when specific materials are required. Long lead items can be identified. Plant requirements can be identified and of course so can labour and sub-contractors. The realistic programme has a lot to offer.

5.1.11 How Do We Ensure The Programme Is Realistic?

Experience will indicate how long each task will take to complete. If say the plumber says he will first fix a house in a day – is it realistic to provide one day for this task? At first it would appear that it would be realistic – given that this is the length of time it will take. However, if say a five day period is provided for the first fix, clearly setting out the first day that the work can be commenced, and the day that the mechanical contractor must be completed for the next trade to move in – which is the most realistic? If there is a bit of flexibility built into the scheduling, it gives everyone, including the Site Manager, a bit of breathing space, and if a day is lost it won't affect the programme. If however the single day is provided that he asked for, it puts everybody under intense pressure. If a day is lost in these circumstances – all following dates will be altered and the whole programme for that house will suffer. Providing five days to do one days work might seem like a luxury that can't be afforded, but I would much prefer to build flexibility into the programme. The secret to getting a scheme of houses built rapidly is not based on tying the mechanical contractor down to the day – but on getting him to first fix five houses over a five-day period if each one takes one day to complete.

The obvious danger attached to a five day window to do a day's work – is that the Site Manager has to ensure that the work is completed within that window and that the sub-contractor involved doesn't keep turning up on the fifth day to do the work.

When the first draft of the programme is prepared, the Site Manager should sit down with other on site management personnel, and study the draft carefully. The following points should be addressed:

- Can this much work be done at the same time? It is very easy to programme work on paper, but is it practical on the ground?
- Will the building hold that many people at the same time? Again it is easy to programme twenty gangs in the one house at the one time, but we all know that, unless it is a huge house, twenty gangs couldn't work in the house at once. They would simply be in each other's way and production would be virtually nil.
- Can we service that much work at one time? Again it looks great on paper but has the firm the resources to

service that much work at once? There may be issues of forklifts, access, power etc.

- Can each sub-contractor do that much work at once? Is the programme achievable from the sub-contractors point of view? Has he the manpower, tools, plant and other resources to achieve what is required?
- Can we supervise that much work at one time? By no means an insignificant consideration. If there are sub-contractors and direct workers in action all over the site, is there adequate supervision to maintain quality?

With a printout of the programme before him – the Site Manager should draw a vertical line down through the busiest part of the programme and visualise the work scheduled for that time. Keeping in mind the above points, he will know there and then if the programme is realistic. This is also the time to make any changes.

5.1.12 Delivering The Programme.

The Site Manager should at all time push for rigid adherence to the programme. He should take action at the first sign of slippage. Sub-Contractors who are genuinely causing a delay, should be called in to a special meeting to discuss the problem and the Site Manager should make it clear that he will tolerate no further delays. All avenues should be explored to find a solution to the existing delay, and the Site Manager should in conjunction with the Contracts Manager or Director in charge, line-up a substitute sub-contractor to complete the works. This substitute should be engaged and the problematic one removed from the site, if the problem recurs.

Programme slippage should not be allowed to delay the handover date. In a housing project, time lost in one house should be confined to that house, and the commencement of next one should go ahead as planned. Delays should be ring-fenced in the area where they occurred.

At the outset of this book we listed "On Time" as a key site-management function. The programme will indicate the time and ultimately it is the Site Manager, not the sub-contractors or other workers who delivers it. There is no room for sentiment when the programme starts to slip, and there will be no shelter in the storm for the Site Manager if he fails to act.

5.2   Progress Reports

Progress reports serve a number of purposes. They are very important for head office and for the client, to keep track on the job. But they are very useful for the Site Manager too. By preparing regular progress reports he can monitor how each trade and each task is progressing. He can identify ongoing problems and is armed with facts rather that hearsay or opinion, when he tackles the problem.

When the Site Manager is asked to prepare a progress report he should consider its implications very carefully. On the surface it is a written record of the progress of work on the site. But the shrewd Site Manager won't rush into writing this up. As with anything the Site Manager puts in writing, there are a number of considerations to be kept in mind.

Who will read the report? If it is for the client, is there any danger that what the Site Manager puts in writing will contradict something that someone else has been telling the client? Maybe the QS has submitted a claim for total payment for something that is not one hundred percent completed. It has been know to happen. If the Site Manager states in his progress report, something which is different from the claim for payment, then this inconsistency could cause a cheque to be delayed and may have serious consequences for cash-flow.

If the report is for head office, is there any particular complexion that the Site Manager may want to put on it? Does Head Office need to know the exact position? There may be times when the Site Manager feels it is in both his, and the best interests of the job, that head office is not fully aware of the true and accurate position. Perhaps something, which was due to be fully completed, while not absolutely completed, is as good as, and will be finished before the progress report reaches head office.   What should the Site Manager put in his report for this? Whatever way he chooses to play it, the Site Manager should be aware that as the saying goes, honesty is the best policy, and you have to have a super memory to be an effective liar.

5.2.1 Preparing the Report

A relatively easy way to prepare a progress report is to list the tasks that have been commenced and estimate a percentage of each task completed. Unfortunately this report is virtually useless as the information it provides is severely limited.

The progress report should indicate actual progress versus expected (programmed) progress. It should compare where the job is at, with where the job should be at, at that time.

To do this the Site Manager should list in the progress report, each item as it appears on the programme, and then fill in the programmed start and completion dates, and the programmed duration. Next, he should then enter columns for the actual start date, actual finish date and actual duration. Finally, for tasks incomplete, he should add in the revised start and/or completion dates and duration. A column showing any differences, plus or minus, in days will complete the report. Most computer software programmes designed for programming works can prepare these reports, but the Site Manager who is not comfortable with computers can do this manually himself, on a sheet or sheets of paper. (See sample progress report Schedule 3 at the rear of this book.)

This method of tracking progress identifies slippage or acceleration immediately, and gives the Site Manager an opportunity to intervene to get the programme back on track, or whatever he wishes. It gives him real factual data on which he can make an informed choice.

There is another use for the type of progress report discussed above.

If the contractor is finding it difficult to obtain information from the client or his representatives, this type of progress report is a very useful tool for a claim. The contractor will be able to demonstrate that task A should have commenced on say the 19th of January, but couldn't be commenced until the 26th because of late detail. The delay may filter down through the job and, if it was on the critical path, may result in the contractor having to spend more time on the site that was originally estimated. He may be able to claim payment for the extra time on site.

Building Chemicals

Construction Accessories stock a large range of chemicals for use in construction:

- Release Agents
- Curing Agents
- Retarders
- Grouts
- Repair Mortars
- Waterproofing
- Bonding agents

Waterstops

- Water bar – internally and externally cast.
- Hydrophillic strip – swells on contact with water

External waterstop 1

**Construction Accessories Ltd
Toughers Industrial Estate
Newhall, Naas,
Co. Kildare
Tel: 045-438691 Fax 045-438690
www.constructionaccessories.ie**

Chapter 6 – RESOURCES

Resources in summary are the <u>finance</u>, <u>people</u>, <u>plant</u>, <u>equipment</u>, <u>permits</u>, <u>time</u> and <u>materials</u> needed to do the job. The planning, scheduling and management of resources are some of the primary functions of a Site Manager. From a head office point of view, resources equals costs, and much of what the Site Manager will require will be viewed by head office – as just that – a cost. But to a large degree, head office is right because resources are costs and are directly chargeable against the job and against the profit margin. And after all the primary duty of any business, construction included, is to make a profit. That's why firms exist.

The Site Manager has to plan carefully what resources he will need, when he will need them, what additional costs (resources) will be required to maintain or use them, and how they are to be managed while on site.

6.1   Consult The Programme

The first port of call for the Site Manager in determining his resourcing requirements is the programme. The programme lists all of the jobs to be undertaken, and their start and completion dates. By reading down through the tasks it is easy to see exactly *what* is needed, *when* and for *how long*. But the management of the resources and the additional costs, which may be incurred along the way, needs careful attention to prevent wastage.

If the site does not enjoy the luxury of some form of relevant programme then the Site Manager has two options. He can compile a programme in some fashion, or he can keep making it up as he goes along. He may not have time to do the former to get him out of the position he is now in, but continuation of the latter ("fire-fighting") is a recipe for certain disaster. The Site Manager who doesn't have – or won't compile a programme, would be well advised to spend a bit of time getting his cv together because he will almost certainly need it before long.

Assuming that the programme exists, the Site Manager needs to satisfy himself that:

- The programme is on time,
- All of the tasks are included,
- The timeframe (Duration) allocated to each task is reasonable and achievable,
- That the overlapping tasks can be physically carried out simultaneously.

If the programme has slipped, the Site Manager can still use it by "moving it along" that is - changing the dates. Excluded tasks can be factored in, but the knock-on effects of these omissions must be studied carefully. If the time allocation is inadequate he must adjust this and re-examine the knock-on effects, and at all times he must be conscious of the physical limitations of the site, in terms of working space and safety. Finally if the programme needed any adjustment along the lines of the above, the Site Manager needs to get his hands on an updated programme immediately.

Additional items not immediately visible on the programme must be taken into account. If the Site Manager identifies a need for some item of plant, for example, he must remember that he may need fuel for the plant and that in turn means that he will need drums or storage for the fuel and a local supplier will need to be selected. When the programme identifies scaffolding requirements, the Site Manager may need to examine carefully what *exactly* will be needed. Perhaps there will be a requirement for more "two-board brackets" or some other specific component. It is dangerous to assume that there is adequate scaffolding on site, unless the Site Manager is fully aware of exactly what is needed *and* what is on site.

The Site Manager should go through his programme carefully every week and keep on top of all resource requirements. Many accidents can be attributed to using the wrong equipment for a specific job, and often poor planning is the cause of the shortage of the correct equipment.

6.2   Materials – The "Three Day Rule"

Many firms operate what is called the "three-day rule." If

the site needs a particular item, be it materials plant or equipment, the requisition is sent to head office three days before the particular item is required. This gives the purchasing department a bit of breathing space to source at the best price, and gives the merchant a bit of breathing space to deliver. The three day rule is simple enough for a site to operate too, as even the most disorganised sites have an idea of what they will be doing in there days time. Failure to operate the three day rule will leave the purchasing department vulnerable to paying top price for something – simply because it is available *now,* rather than checking prices and terms and selecting the most suitable supplier.

Some firms of course leave it to the site to source materials and operate an "order book" or worse still an "order number" system from site. <u>This is a disastrous practice</u>, as <u>it exposes the firm to paying virtually any price for any item, simply because of convenience</u> or availability. If, however, this practice exists, it is another function that has to be managed by the Site Manager.

It is my opinion that <u>the sourcing of all materials should be carried out by a purchasing department, which is separate from the site.</u> This purchasing department should liaise with all sites, and should be a key player in the management of cash flow in the company.

If the sourcing of materials function is left to the site to carry out, then the Site Manager has a huge additional task to manage. He will need to keep strict control on the order book, and need a very reliable man to send "shopping" for materials. The Site Manager will need to build up a rapport with the merchants (or their representatives) that he is dealing with, and monitor the invoices closely to see that all is in order. Unscrupulous traders unfortunately do exist, and <u>construction companies channelling their purchasing function through their sites are a very easy target for fraud.</u>

A system for control of purchases will have to be put in place on the site, consisting of the following: Requisition, Order, Delivery Note, Goods Received Docket. *(See diagram on the following page.)*

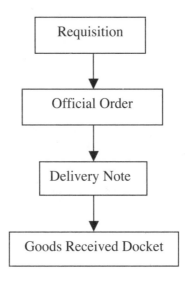

The Site Manager should ensure that these steps are completed and in the correct order for each order placed. This is the paper trail and while many managers will be dismissive of paperwork, the above procedures are essential for keeping track of what is bought on the site. These documents are discussed in more detail in Chapter 2.

6.3   Scheduling

Some firms do all of the purchasing before the job commences or very close to the commencement date, and leave it to site to "call-off" or schedule the material as it is required. Again the Site Manager needs to be thinking three days ahead at least, as the supplier will not be able to deliver at the drop of a hat.

The Site Manager needs to keep track of how much of the total bulk-order has been called-off for each item and how this relates to the percentage of work completed involving that particular item. Materials can be wasted on sites and can disappear during and after working hours. It makes sense to call in materials at a sensible rate to prevent this "shrinkage." Of course this won't always be possible due to transport and perhaps packaging constraints. This is an area where tight management is required and particular attention should be paid to it.

6.4 Long Lead Items

Long lead items need special attention because of their nature. Windows, lift cars, fitted furniture etc are examples of items which are not available "off the shelf." The Site Manager needs to liase with the relevant suppliers or specialist contractors, examine carefully their lead-time and examine the programme requirements, checking for potential problems. Once this is sorted he needs to frequently ring-up the suppliers to keep them focused on the scheduled delivery dates, and alert himself to any potential delays. Most situations can be worked around, once the Site Manager is aware that there may be a problem. The real problems occur when everyone is standing up waiting for some particular item, which three months ago was promised for delivery today. When the truck isn't on site by breakfast time the Site Manager rings up to discover that the item hasn't been manufactured yet. One way of solving this is to make a reminder note in the site diary, to call the supplier at regular intervals perhaps weekly or fortnightly.

If a delay is envisaged, the Site Manager needs to carry out a realistic appraisal of the implications of the delay and assess its impact on other elements of the job. To take the installation of the lift car as an example, a delay of two weeks may have no real impact on finishing or handover dates, or it may delay other trades like decorators who have to work on each floor tidying up around the doors to the lift, depending on the programme.

6.5 Credit Period

The purchasing department will have negotiated a credit period with suppliers and the Site Manager should take this into account when "calling-off" or requisitioning materials. This means not taking in a huge quantity of materials near the month end.

Materials should generally be taken in at the beginning of the month for that month and the next consignment coming in at the beginning of the following month. This management of the credit terms can be very advantageous to the contractor. Of course the Site Manager may not need to take in a month's supply at one time depending on the materials and site in question, but he certainly should avoid taking in more than a month's supply, unless there is some other good reason for doing so.

The Site Manager will not always be able to stick to this principle but he should be keep it in mind as cash-flow is crucial to the smooth running of any business.

Sometimes issues surrounding the credit period can be the cause of a delay, the purchasing department having "held-off" an order for a few days, to gain another month's credit. Where this happens it is only fair that purchasing would inform the Site Manager accordingly, so that there is no resultant delay on site. If the "holding-off" is genuinely unacceptable to the Site Manager he should inform purchasing.

6.6   Storage

Storage is a resource in itself and most sites won't have an unlimited amount of it. A storage plan should be in place even if this is only verbally agreed between the interested parties. The man in charge of goods inwards, often the forklift driver, should be made aware of the likely deliveries so that storage practices can be controlled and space utilised. When orders are placed or called off, the delivery dates should be agreed, and the man in charge of goods-in should be kept briefed.

Unchecked, unsuitable, faulty or damaged goods should be stored in a specially designated area. See Chapter 11.

Care should be taken with storage of materials. Obviously some items will not benefit from exposure to rain or dampness. Hollowcore concrete units need special care as they can snap at the skids, if any additional weight put on them. Lengths of timber can twist if stored incorrectly. Roof trusses need careful storage. Safety must be foremost in the mind of the person in charge of materials storage – materials can fall, even long after they have been stored apparently "safely." In addition, consideration must be given to the order in which materials are to be used, as this is rarely the order in which materials arrive to site.

6.7   Approval.

Some clients may require samples of materials or finishes for approval prior to use, or may need written notification of the supplier that the contractor intends to use. This may often be a formality but can come back to haunt the Site Manager if shortcuts are taken or procedures aren't followed. Light fittings, tiles, sanitary ware, etc., are all examples of typical products where samples may need approval. It is very important that samples are not mixed in with other, similar, materials which may have received prior approval or not need approval.

The Site Manager should read the specifications and contract documentation fully, to alert himself to items, procedures, sub-contractors or suppliers needing prior approval. Obviously, he needs to do his research into the most suitable choice from the contractor's view, prior to nomination.

Communication to all interested parties is important. Some form of identification procedure should be put in place to identify items awaiting approval. This may be the marking off of a certain area for storage of samples with appropriate signage, or some form of labelling of the items themselves. Whatever method is used, it is important that some method is used. Sub contractors will be seeking payment for placing the unapproved materials, and the nuisance value alone of fighting with subcontractors over the use of unapproved materials should be sufficient deterrent alone for the Site Manager.

6.8   Certification

Some clients will seek certification for materials used and some certification will be needed for the Safety File. Accordingly the Site Manager should seek all documentation relating to the products used and these should be filed away carefully. When approval is received this should be confirmed in writing and any documentation involved should be filed away safely.

In the case of items used everyday, like cement, blocks, bricks, timber, etc, the Site Manager should prepare a file with the relevant documentation which he can bring with him from site to site.

6.9   Personnel

When the Site Manager studies the programme he will have a good indication of the number of people he will need on the site at the various stages of the job. The majority of these will probably be sub-contractors, some may be agency labour and the balance will be employed directly. He will also calculate the requirements for engineers, technicians, surveyors, drivers, finishing foremen etc. Head office will have "taken for" these requirements in the Prelims, but the two figures may not always tally. The normal sequence of events is that the Site Manager notifies head office of his requirements and their reaction is: What do you want all that for? Like most things they will see people as a cost eating away into the bottom line.

The most common method of calculating the personnel requirements is to study each task to be undertaken and to figure out from that how many people will be required. This brings us right back to the programme.

Personnel on site need back-up resources like welfare facilities, car park spaces, tools and equipment, etc. These considerations should be studied carefully before the Site Manager floods the site with people. He should also keep in mind that all personnel on the site will need instruction and supervision. Sometimes it isn't just a case of getting more people on board.

6.10   Plant & Equipment

Plant and equipment requirements are normally calculated again from the list of jobs in the programme. Some plant will require specialist operators or drivers. Where this is the case these drivers may need certification under the Fás Construction Skills programme (CSCS.) The full list is attached in Schedule 4 at the rear of this book.

Where scaffolding is required, this will need to be erected by a competent person again with appropriate certification. Scaffolding is a major issue for any site and one of the first things the HSA Representative will look at on a site visit. The Site Manager should take no short cuts with scaffolding irrespective of the pressures applied for speedy construction or the costs involved. If an accident occurs the focus will be back on the Site Manager and claims that "the pressure was on to get the job done" or " we hadn't enough gear" will provide no hiding place from responsibility. No Site Manager will want to be the cause of, or significant contributor to, a fatality.

When calling in plant the Site Manager will want to carefully consider how much work can physically be done simultaneously. There is no point in having plant on site standing idle because there is insufficient room to work. Like the manpower requirements – sometimes flooding the site with plant is not the answer either!

It is important to devise a method of working and this is best decided after discussion with other interested parties. Taking the case of drainage as an example, it might be wise to discuss the options with the pipe-layers before deciding where to commence. This will determine how much plant can physically work in one place at the one time. Once the Site Manager makes the decision he should communicate it clearly to all involved and should act swiftly if the crew on the ground decide to do something else.

6.11   Permits

This might seem an unlikely item under resources but permits are often required before certain works can proceed. Road opening permits may be required from the local authority before connections can be made to services. In addition tipping of spoil from the site is another item now requiring permits. Disposal of asbestos or other hazardous materials will require special permits and these permits will have to be obtained before progress can be made.

The Site Manager should ensure that permits are applied for on time and that the permit has been granted before work commences. The Site Manager should check the permit carefully – sometimes it may contain restrictions or conditions which could have an impact on how or when the job can be done. The permit or a copy, should be filed on site and available for inspection by any relevant parties.

While on the subject of permits the Site Manager should check the contract documents to see if there are restrictions on working hours or restrictions on specific type of works.

6.12 Consumables

Consumables are a resource which is frequently overlooked on sites. PPE, hygiene supplies, stationary, blades, cutting and grinding discs, drills, nails, screws, fixings, fuel (including drums) etc., will all be required and must be requisitioned or scheduled just like materials. Equally these items need appropriate storage and management to prevent wastage.

6.13 Temporary Works

Temporary works can eat up a colossal amount of money if not kept in check. Temporary works may include the following:
- Supply, installation and later removal of a septic tank or tanks for temporary toilets or a connection to the sewer.
- Some formwork/false-work and relevant materials.
- Supply, erection, painting and maintenance of hoarding.
- Polythene or other covering for protection of work.
- Pumps, pipes and fittings for disposal of ground water.
- Mobilisation and demobilisation.
- Electricity for the cabins etc for the duration of the contract.
- Signage.

Expansion Joint Materials

Construction Accessories stock a wide range of expansion joint materials suitable for use with brick, block and concrete, for general construction and civil engineering applications.

- Joint strip
- Wood fibre filler board
- Foam rod
- Miothene 70
- Slip membranes
- Bitucork
- Corktex

 - Joint foam with tear strip

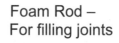

Foam Rod – For filling joints

For finishing joints, sealants are also available:

- Two part polysulphide
- One part polyurethane
- Chemical resistant sealants
- Fire resistant sealants
- All in a variety of colours

Construction Accessories Ltd
Toughers Industrial Estate
Newhall, Naas,
Co. Kildare
Tel: 045-438691 Fax 045-438690
www.constructionaccessories.ie

Chapter 7 – PEOPLE MANAGEMENT

7.1   Dealing With People – Generally

The ability to successfully deal with people is an essential quality in a Site Manager. Giving and receiving instructions, dealing with labour relations issues, appeasing distraught neighbours, listening to whingeing sub-contractors, politely escorting trespassers from the site – the list of situations where the Site Manager has to interact with others is almost endless.

It is important that the Site Manager remains cool under pressure – because under pressure he will frequently be.

7.2   Trust & Respect

Two of the key factors that dictate how we deal with people are trust and respect. Both have to be earned. Respect usually operates at a very conscious level while trust frequently operates at a sub-conscious level. Trust and respect are very important considerations for the Site Manager.

Many people think that workers should automatically trust and respect their superiors. If this were the case, once the Site Manager walked out on to the site for the first time, all workers and sub-contractors would trust him instantly, and act out of respect for him immediately. In reality however, it is more likely that, while they wouldn't be deliberately disrespectful, they certainly wouldn't immediately trust him, and would proceed with caution and check him out over time. Even then, and presuming that the workforce "took to him" instantly, and if he lived up to their expectations, it would still take a long time to build trust and respect.

Respect of course should always be a two way process. The Site Manager should have respect for the workers too. And when he walks out on to that site for the first time, while he probably will have a fair deal of respect for them, it is unlikely that this exact measure will be maintained after he gets to know them. Some will go up in his esteem - maybe others will go down.

Trust on the other hand, doesn't exist at all in that first meeting. Certainly, meaningful trust doesn't anyway. Trust is built up incrementally over time.

The Site Manager should be cautious about accepting everyone at face value and should be especially careful with other colleagues at management level. Most managers in most organisations have an "agenda" and the Site Manager should build his own relationships and place his trust carefully.

The famous Machiavellian quote "keep your friends close and your enemies even closer" comes to mind.

7.3   Ownership of Problems.

In order to get tasks completed, it is very important for the Site Manager to be generally aware of the whole issue of "ownership" of problems. When someone comes along to the Site Manager and says for example, "I can't do this task because I don't have a drill" the manager could respond by saying "I'll get one to you in a few minutes" or he could say "go to the stores and get the drill from the shelf." The critical difference in the two responses is just _who_ is responsible for the next action. In the first response the Site Manager took over ownership of the problem. "I'll get one to you..." This was in effect saying, "you do nothing until I get the drill to you." The whole issue of finding the drill and delivering it was "taken-on" by the Site Manager. In the second response, the Site Manager firmly placed responsibility for the next action with the person who brought the problem to him in the first place. The drill is only one example. It can be shortage of materials, lack of information, a follow up phone call. The critical point for the Site Manager is to identify the problem, and delegate responsibility – not to take on the problem – himself.

As an aid to recognition of these situations, I always identify the problem as the "pup." Pups are generally soft, playful and cuddly, and are generally well liked, except by people who detest dogs anyway. When someone comes to him with a problem, the Site Manager should visualise that problem as a pup. He should ensure that when the discussion is concluded that the pup remains with the person who brought it to him in the first place. Pups need to be fed, they seek attention, and aren't toilet trained. To make matters worse, they grow into dogs. Dogs with hefty appetites, and sometimes, malodours and foul tempers. Problems unnecessarily "taken-on" by the Site Manager, usually adopt similar, unwelcome characteristics.

Don't collect pups.

7.4   Dealing with the workers on site.

The Site Manager is responsible for getting the job done but of course he is not expected to do it all himself. The following is a list of points the Site Manager should keep in mind when dealing with workers on the site, as he goes about the daily task of getting the job done.

- Define clear goals. Break big tasks into smaller ones – the end to which can clearly be visualised. Nothing is worse that trying to make a far away target seem real or relevant.
- Tasks should be clearly assigned, with everyone aware of what's expected. Ensure the message is sent to everyone involved.
- Check to make sure the message is understood. This is particularly relevant with workers who's first language is not English.
- The Site Manager should not accept "no" for an answer. "No" can come in may forms – a laugh, a shake of the head or a smile, but a "no" won't get the job done.
- Failure to meet one target cannot be allowed to effect the next one or the overall goal. If a target isn't met, it should be dealt with in isolation. There is no future in letting one missed deadline delay the overall job.
- The Site Manager should form his own opinions regarding individual ability and performance. He should not dismiss someone on the basis of hearsay. Equally, he should decide for himself if someone is as good as he says he is, or his friends claim.

- Keep in mind that *everyone* has something to add and to offer. Sometimes the Site Manager may have to look a bit deeper that at other times.
- Listen to workers, their concerns, fears and opinions. Much can be learned about the way they see things.
- Offer support when things aren't going so well. Some workers may have family problems or something similar. The Site Manager should give them a hearing and if he can help – he should do so.
- Encourage workers to perform – rather than instruct, or worst of all – threaten. Use persuasion and influence to encourage self-motivation.
- Show loyalty to workers. They will be much more likely to be loyal in return.
- Don't look for perfection – look for reality and honesty. If their effort is good enough, say so.
- Praise work well done. Don't just take it for granted, expect it, or adopt he attitude of "that's what they're there for." It is very easy to criticise.
- Check errors, without making a scene. Don't let quality slip for the sake of being a "nice guy."
- Be tough on the problem – not the person. There is a big difference.
- Avoid personal attacks.
- Ensure that workers have adequate resources to get the job done. This is a key issue. If they haven't got the right tools plant or materials – it is really harder and slower to deliver. Don't expect too much improvisation.
- Keep work varied. Maybe this can be achieved by switching personnel around on the one task or by changing tasks.
- Defuse disputes instantly. Don't let them develop into ongoing battles. If necessary change the team – but once a dispute comes to the Site Manager's attention, he must deal with without taking sides.

- Troublemakers should be dealt with the instant that awareness of their existence becomes apparent. If necessary get them off the site. Watch out not to infringe their rights.
- Beware of signs of de-motivation and investigate its cause. Absenteeism, cynicism, slow progress can be signs of de-motivation. Stand back and review what the causes may be, and don't be afraid to ask.
- Be decisive. Don't dither. This has its roots in planning, if he knows what the next few moves are it is much easier for the Site Manager to be decisive.
- Deal with the *cause* of problems – not the *symptoms*.

7.5   Employers

The Site Manager will have to be able to deal successfully with his employers. Their perspective will often be totally different from his. On some occasions, head office will seem downright unreasonable to the site and the Manager. Often the Site Manager will just need to be a good listener and keep his cool – let them blow off steam – and get on with the job when they leave.

If he is unlucky enough to have his employer – his boss, on the site all of the time, he again should get on with his job and run the site as if the boss wasn't there. The boss probably has many other things to be worrying about, than the day-to-day running of the site. If the boss starts to interfere in the day-to-day issues, or gives instructions to workers inconsistent with the instruction issued by the Site Manager, then a huge problem exists. Sub-contractors and workers will manipulate the situation to their advantage. The Site Manager will feel undermined and will be in an impossible situation. In these circumstances the Site Manager should seek a meeting with his boss, and explain the situation. The boss may not have been aware that he was becoming involved, or that his actions were undermining the Site Manager. Perhaps his motivation was merely offering assistance. If this doesn't resolve the situation, the Site Manager should start looking around for other employment opportunities, and when a suitable position is found, should move on.

7.6   Sub Contractors

Some sub-contractors tend as a general rule to whinge a bit and look for excuses for "day-works" or extras. The Site Manager has to be firm in his approach but can avoid some of the arguments by making sure that the work is ready for the sub-contractor. Sub contractors are dealt with in some detail in Chapter 8.

The Site Manager should take a firm line with difficult sub-contractors, without being confrontational or aggressive in the process. Many sub-contractors "try it on" with a Site Manager they have not met before, but if they find him firm and fair, the Site Manager can often enjoy a peaceful time with the sub-contractor, most of the time, thereafter.

Many of the topics listed in the section on dealing with the workers on site, above, are relevant to sub-contractors.

One final point on sub-contractors. The day the Site Manager accepts money as a gift from a sub-contractor, is the day the Site Manager has lost control of the site, and with it, all credibility. The offer of monetary gifts from sub-contractors at Christmas or other holiday time, is common within the industry, and the Site Manager should never, ever, accept the money, irrespective of how small or large the amount, or the circumstances involved.

7.7   Design Team

Dealing with the design team can be very straightforward or can be quite tricky, depending on the job and the people involved. The Site Manager should be professional and courteous in his dealing with people at all times, especially, perhaps, in his dealing with the design team and the client. His first responsibility, after his family and personal priorities, is of course to his employers, so he won't want to let the design team "walk on him." But why would they want to do that? Well they probably won't, but since the contractor has tendered for the job and won it because his price was acceptable – he won't want to be delayed in getting on with it.

Designers frequently change details during the contract period, and sometimes the contractor can't get paid for the extra time involved. The changes might appear to be relatively simple, and in isolation, probably are. However, if the change were to internal door types for example, the original ones may have been already ordered from the manufacturer. The existing doorframes might be unsuitable for the different door type, or the door furniture may be unsuited to the new door. The proposed alternative may be slower to work with, the material used on the outer face of the door may be softer and require extra care, or the priming and painting requirements may be different. So while the designers might simply wish to change the door style or type, the implications may go much further for the contractor. The change above may require re-ordering, and doors may be a long lead item. If the doorframes need to be changed, these again may be already ordered or may have been installed in the first fix. If they are installed will the client pay for their removal and replacement? The door furniture may be more expensive, and/or difficult to source. If the door skin is of a softer wood than originally priced, there may be a greater risk of damage to the doors during installation or afterwards, before the building is handed over. The finishing requirements may have cost implications for the contractor.

The Site Manager, as the contractor's representative on site, has to consider all the implications of any proposed changes and have the vision to identify which ones suit the contractor and which ones don't. He has to be able to deter the designers from the unsuitable changes, or "steer" them in the direction of the ones he wants – without offending anybody in the process, and, to use a card-playing term, without showing his hand.

Many Site Managers complain of indecision in individual members of the design team. The Clerk of Works or the Resident Engineer may be unauthorised to make "on the spot" decisions, and individuals from the architects or consulting engineering firm may be unwilling to do so. This inertia can be very frustrating for the Site Manager wishing to push on with the job, often under duress to do so from his own head office. Indeed it is commonly perceived by contractors that the designers slow up the construction process considerably. For their part, designers commonly believe the opposite – that contractors are always in a rush, unwilling to accept that the design element takes time and attention. As a project develops, clients sometimes change their minds on specific requirements, resulting in re-design, for which the architect or consulting engineer frequently get no additional fees.

It is probably fair to say that designers do sometimes hold up the job, but the Site Manager should understand the cultural differences, which exist between designers and contractors. It isn't always incompetence or laziness on the part of the designers.

The Site Manager should bear in mind that difficulties with the design team are not always straightforward, and that life can be tough for them too.

7.8   Client

Management of the client is a tricky job and one requiring great care. He is, after all, the one paying for the whole job and the wages and salaries of everyone engaged on it, so he is entitled to some say in how it turns out. The Site Manager should at all times be courteous towards the client.

The design team will take instructions from the client and offer advice. In theory neither the Site Manager nor any other representative of the contracting firm should have any direct dealings on a day-to-day basis with the client. In reality however, the client frequently gets involved directly with the contractor, and may order wholesale changes to both completed works and works not yet commenced. The Site Manager is in a similar position to that with the design team as described above, and has to use all his diplomatic skills to appease the client without conceding ground.

7.9   End-Users

If you are working on a housing or apartment development, you may be required to meet the eventual customers or end-users. They may be seeking changes, or specific finishes. The Site Manager should remember who it is that is paying his employers – usually a developer, and bear in mind that the contract is between them, and not the eventual users. Issues regarding specific apartments or houses may be outside his brief and if he takes these proposed changes on board, he may be acting outside his authority and may end up with a whole load of extra work for which nobody is prepared to pay.

Alternatively this may be included in the Site Managers brief, and he may be required to liaise with the end-users regarding finishes. He should at all times keep his opinions to himself, listen carefully to what is requested, check to see if it is an approved option and get the end-users to sign a record of the request. The documentation should be forwarded immediately to the client (developer) and to head office. End-users have been known to deny they made certain requests, if the finished article is not as appealing as originally envisioned. There will always be a cut-off point in the construction of any project, after which time, it is too late to make changes. There may be different cut-off points for different elements of the job, and the Site Manager should notify the end-users when they visit the site or show-house, when the relevant dates are. He should not, however, go calling on buyers, seeking clarification of requirements. The rules of the game should be explained to the end users early on, and should be done so by the auctioneer or the client himself. The Site Manager should not shy away from politely explaining the situation to the end-users, in an effort to get an early decision on the options.

It is vital that all options selected are signed off by the end-user, even if head office or the client don't require this practice to be carried-out.

7.10   Suppliers

The purchasing department will normally select suppliers, and the Site Manager may have little involvement with them on a day-to-day basis, other than accepting deliveries to the site. Where the Site Manager has regular involvement with suppliers the following should be borne in mind.

Suppliers are normally perceived as the least important group of people to be dealt with. There is the inaccurate assumption that since the company chooses the supplier, and that since money changes hands, the supplier can be walked on, or will dance to the tune of the contractor every time. The reality is far different, and suppliers, on which the contractor has walked all over, will remember this abuse, and at the first opportunity teach the contractor a lesson.

Suppliers should be viewed as partners in the building process, and their representatives should be treated in a courteous and professional manner at all times. Adequate notice of requirements should be given to the supplier (see "Three Day Rule" – Chapter Six) and unreasonable delivery demands should be avoided where possible. It is likely that the supplier will be more willing to meet he unreasonable delivery demand if he is treated with respect rather that being expected to jump when the contractor shouts.

Finally, the Site Manager should never accept a gift of money from a supplier, as with sub-contractors.

7.11　Visitors

Procedures should be put in place to intercept any visitors to the site, from progressing past the entrance gate. There is any number of reasons why visitors should be prevented from roaming the site at their discretion, from health and safety considerations to security risks.

There may be genuine reasons for visits – indeed most visitors have a valid reason for calling. The visitor might be a relative of one of the workers for example, or a supplier to a sub-contractor. Alternatively the visitor may be unwelcome – his motivation for calling may be disruptive, or he may be on a research mission for a later theft.

If the site has a security officer, he should be detailed on the procedure for dealing with visitors. Irrespective of who actually deals with the visitor, politeness and courtesy should be used, even if he is suspicious looking.

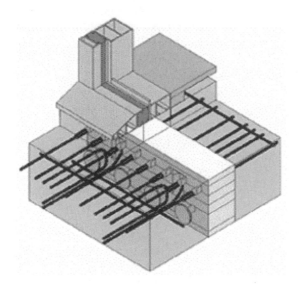

Chapter 8 – SUB-CONTRACTORS.

Specialist Sub Contractors are appointed to almost every project in the construction industry. These may be suppliers of a particular product, or may be designers, manufacturers and installers. The use of sub-contractors is widespread throughout the industry, and the management of sub-contractors is one of the biggest challenges facing the Site Manager.

8.1   Domestic and Nominated

Sub-contractors initially fall into two categories – domestic and nominated. The main contractor chooses domestic sub-contractors, and their appointment may need ratification by the client, depending on the type of job, or the terms of the main contract.

Nominated sub contractors are suppliers or specialist sub-contractors nominated by the architect or the client, and as such the contractor has, in reality, very little choice other than to work with them. Once appointed, nominated sub-contractors fall into the same category as domestic sub-contractors, in terms of on site management.

8.2   The Pre-Appointment Meeting

The procurement of sub-contractors is often outside the control of the Site Manager, the process having begun at tendering stage and continued up to the point of the sub-contractor visiting the site prior to appointment. The Site Manager should insist on an input on the sub-contractor selection process and at the very least should hold a pre-appointment meeting. The pre appointment meeting is critical in the management of sub-contractors and will have a bearing on the quality and satisfaction of the sub-contractor's performance. The importance of the pre-appointment meeting cannot be over stressed.

The purpose of the pre appointment meeting is to agree the rules of engagement, prior to the signing of the contract. If the meeting goes ahead and the sub-contractor is subsequently appointed, then the outcome of the meeting will form part of the contract and have legal implications. It is therefore of vital importance that the meeting is properly structured and minuted.

It is useful to have a form prepared in advance of the pre-appointment meeting, with spaces provided for the following items, some of which will be standard to all sub-contracts and can be completed in advance. The contents of the form will form the agenda for the meeting and will form part of the contract. While there may be slight variations from one firm to the next, the following should be included at a minimum:

- The name and address of the principal contractor.
- The name and address of the sub-contractor.
- The name and telephone number of the person within the main contracting firm, dealing with the contract. This might be a Contracts Manager, or a Director.
- The name of the person within the main contracting firm, handling the financial side of the account. The person will issue the vouchers for payment.
- The name and telephone number of the person within the sub-contracting firm, dealing with the contract. This might be a Contracts Manager, or a Director or a foreman on the site.
- The name and telephone number of the person within the sub-contracting firm, to whom instructions can be given on site.
- Full particulars of the nature of the proposed works to be carried out, materials to be supplied etc.
  - o This usually takes the form of a list of the documents, which the sub-contractor has already priced, unless some part of the original works is not proceeding, or is otherwise omitted.
  - o Associated omissions should also be noted. This might include, say, glazing, in the case of a window supplier, if he were supplying the windows – but not the glazing.
- Particulars of the main contract including:

- o Defects Liability Period.
- o Method of Measurement.
- o Completion Date.
- o Liquidated and Ascertained Damages.
- o Period of Interim Certificates.
- Sub-Contract Particulars:
  - o Form of Agreement.
  - o Value of Sub-Contract Works.
  - o Discount – if any.
  - o Period of Interim Payment – some sub-contractors will be happy with payment at the end of the following month, others will need payment much sooner.
  - o Retention. The main contractor should insist on holding some retention on the sub-contractor. The period and amount of retention, will be the subject of negotiation, but some retention should be held.
  - o Price Variation Arrangements. Will additional works be measured and priced in the same manner as the rest of the contract items?
  - o Rates for Dayworks if and where they arise.
  - o Commencement Date.
  - o Completion Date.
- The procedure for determining the contract.
  - o The reasons why the contract would be terminated.
  - o If the contract has to be terminated, the exact procedure for doing so.
  - o This would include details of how the main contractor proposes to have any outstanding works carried out and how the financial aspect of the outstanding work would be dealt with.
- Full particulars of the Sub-Contractor's Insurances. (If the expiry date falls within or close to the completion date of the sub-contract – the Site Manager should make an appropriate note in the site diary a week or so prior to the expiry date, so that he can follow this up at the time.)

- List of Attendances clearly showing which party is responsible for what. This is a very important list and should not be rushed through at the meeting. Items could include:
  - Access roads (Normally the responsibility of the main contractor.)
  - Unloading (Normally the responsibility of the sub-contractor.)
  - Distribution throughout the site. (Normally the responsibility of the sub-contractor.)
  - Hoisting & Lifting. (Normally the responsibility of the sub-contractor.)
  - Storage. (Normally the responsibility of the sub-contractor, but the main contractor would designate a location on site for use by the sub-contractor for storage.)
  - Water Supply (Normally the responsibility of the main contractor.)
  - Waste Bins/Skips (the provision of these is normally the responsibility of the main contractor, but tidying should most definitely be the responsibly of the sub-contractor.)
  - Space for temporary accommodation (Normally the responsibility of the main contractor.)
  - The cabins/offices required for temporary accommodation. (Normally the responsibility of the sub-contractor.)
- Health & Safety
  - A copy of the sub-contractor's Health & Safety Statement should be produced at the meeting and retained on site.
  - A copy of the main contractor's Health & Safety Statement should be presented to the sub-contractor.
  - The site rules regarding the wearing of PPE should be set out by the main contractor. The sub-contractor should be advised in writing, of the costs which will be contra-charged to his account, for items of PPE supplied by the main contractor to the sub-

contractors employees, should they present for work without the appropriate equipment.

- o The dismissal procedure for employees of the sub-contractor, who break the site rules.
- Quality.
    - o The quality standards expected form the sub-contractor should be outlined and the procedure for dealing with outstanding remedial works agreed.
- Programme.
    - o The programme requirements should be outlined and the sub-contractor and a written copy of the relevant dates, or an extract from the programme detailing his works, should be presented to the sub-contractor.
    - o The sub-contractor should be asked if he is able and prepared to proceed with the contract.
    - o If he expresses doubts or says "No," he should not be contracted to do the job.
- Any other item, which in the experience of the Site Manager, or Contracts Manager, should be included.
- Procedures for dealing with problems arising from the sub-contractor's performance on the site, should be discussed at the pre appointment meeting, and fully documented in the contract. This should list the intervention options available to the Site Manager, the notification mechanism and period, and should afford the sub-contractor an opportunity to take corrective action. But the Site Manager should not talk this point down at the meeting – he should not indicate that these items are only listed for "extreme cases" or give any impression that they will be waived. Indeed, the Site Manager should be up front about them and state that they are there to minimise arguments about the hows, whys and wherefores – when he has taken action. The Site Manager must be prepared to act, of course, or the whole process will fail and the sub-contractor, once contracted, will dictate to the Site Manager, rather than the other way around.

8.3 Managing The Sub Contractor On Site

Once the sub-contractor is appointed, management of him and his employees is a matter for the Site Manager. If the pre-appointment meeting has taken place along the lines above, the tools are in place for the Site Manager to deal with issues as they arise. The Site Manager must fulfil his part of the bargain – he must keep the work ahead of the sub-contractor, keep other sub-contractors out of the way, have materials available, or any other promise he has made   But he must not hesitate, or be afraid to act if things are not going according to plan. There is no room for indecision and little room for sentiment when managing a construction site.

8.4 Programme

The Site Manager and his superiors can effectively and legally, deal with any programme slippage, caused by the sub-contractor. It is simply a matter of execution of the procedures set out in the pre-appointment meeting.

8.5 Health & Safety

Once again, the Site Manager and his superiors can rely on the procedures set out at the pre appointment meeting. If operatives turn-up without appropriate PPE, this can be supplied by the main contractor and contra-charged to the sub-contractor's account. After all, the main contractor is only implementing the procedures set out at the pre appointment meeting.

8.6 Quality

Should the quality of the sub-contractor's workmanship suffer, the Site Manager and his superiors have the procedures set out at the pre-appointment meeting to fall back on.   The first option should be to order the remedial work to be undertaken by the sub-contractor himself. This should take the form of a memo to the sub-contractor. This is the first step to a resolution of the problem. Likely outcomes are: -

- Acceptance that something has to be done and the sub-contractor gets on with it. Problem solved.
- Acceptance that something has to be done but the sub-contractor does not get on with it. Another memo is required stating that the Site Manager now intends to instruct someone else to do the job unless the sub-contractor commences the remedial works immediately. If he does – problem solved, if he doesn't – instruct someone immediately as threatened, and record all times and materials involved so that these can be contra-charged to the original sub-contractor's account if so desired.
- Failure to accept that the work is unsatisfactory. The Site Manager should ask himself: Is it unsatisfactory? If he is absolutely sure, then he should point this out to the sub-contractor. The Site Manager could go about this by saying "We won't get away with this" – thereby implying that while he, the Site Manager, understands the sub-contractor's reluctance to accept that the work is in fact of poor quality, the client won't accept the work as it now stands and that something will have to be done. If this doesn't work, a memo should be sent to the sub-contractor informing him that his work is not satisfactory and that a different sub-contractor will be appointed to snag the work, and that all costs involved will be passed on to him. (Don't mention the costs issue unless you know that head office will follow through on it.) If the sub-contractor remains unmoved, then the Site Manager must get Head Office to call in a different sub-contractor – failure to do so will damage his authority and credibility.

Sometimes there may be valid reasons for putting up with poor workmanship, or failing to contra-charge the sub-contractor. After all, this is very much a people industry, and there are any number of situations which could contribute to poor quality. It is important that the Site Manager deals fairly and reasonably with the sub-contractor, and that contra-charges applied don't put him out of business, unless he has been a major problem. Full consideration should be given to quality and programme issues, before the sub-contractor is placed on the tender list as any corrective action at a later stage is both time-consuming and costly, and distracts site management from other tasks.

8.7 Housekeeping

Keeping the place tidy is a constant headache for site management. Sub-contractors will frequently leave debris, materials, even tools and equipment around the place, and happily go home in the evening. One untidy-subcontractor will set the tone for all the others; unfortunately the opposite is not the case.

The Site Manager cannot credibly reprimand one untidy sub-contractor and ignore another. At the first sign of untidiness the Site Manager should pounce, and if the sub-contractor fails to act, then the Site Manager should take action. A number of options may be available to the sub contractor.

Here again, problems can be resolved by implementing the procedures set out at the pre-appointment meeting.

8.8 Problems & Solutions

In fact the solution to all problems, which arise with sub-contractors on site, can be found in the procedures set out at the pre-appointment meeting. The Site Manager will certainly find it easier implementing the rules than making them up as he goes along.

When a special meeting is called with the sub-contractor to iron out problems, the solutions proposed by the Site Manager will not be news to the sub-contractor. After all, he sat down and went through every one of them before he got the job.

It would be foolish however to think that implementation of disciplinary procedures agreed in advance, is the way forward with sub-contractors. In practice, main contractors should simply not ask troublesome sub-contractors to even tender for works, let alone, appoint them.

Successful contractors build up a panel of reliable sub-contractors, within which competitive tendering can take place, any one of which can perform satisfactorily – given the opportunity. The safety net of the pre-appointment meeting, should however, always be in place- just in case.

HALFEN·DEHA
YOUR BEST CONNECTIONS

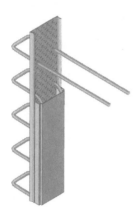 

Continuity Reinforcement

Halfen supply a wide range of reinforcement continuity systems including Kwikastrip, Rebar couplers and Punching shear Reinforcement.

For the full range contact

**Construction Accessories Ltd
Toughers Industrial Estate
Newhall, Naas,
Co. Kildare
Tel: 045-438691 Fax 045-438690
www.constructionaccessories.ie**

Chapter 9 – READING DRAWINGS AND SETTING OUT

Great attention must be paid to drawings. It sounds obvious – but cannot be overstated. Drawings are issued by the architect and consulting engineers, and the contractor is bound to build according to these drawings. It is amazing how much detail can easily be overlooked, if a thorough inspection of drawings is not carried out before any work is commenced. The site engineer, technician and any other on-site professionals or management, should sit in on the review of the drawings – to ensure that all interested parties are briefed. A list of the less obvious features should be written up by the Site Manager, and should be kept in a safe place for cross checking later. Many people find that the process of writing something down in itself, acts as an aid to remembering it again.

The onus is on the firm, as competent contractors, to build what is *designed* – not to build what they think *should* be built. However, if there is an obvious error on a drawing, the contractor must draw the architect or consulting engineer's attention to this fact and seek an agreed solution. The Site Manager should carefully consider the various possible solutions, before drawing attention to the error, and should bear in mind the most advantageous and cost effective solution from the contractor's perspective.

The Site Manager must make himself fully familiar with the drawings for a number of reasons. Obviously he needs to know what has to be built in case anyone else overlooks a seemingly minor feature, but equally he needs to be familiar with all the details for his own credibility as the Site Manager.

9.1   Leaving It To Others.

Most Site Managers leave all setting-out to the site engineer or a technician. This is fine where the Site Manager is familiar with the work of the site engineer or the technician. But what happens if this is the engineer's first job, or his first job with that firm or Site Manager? In other words – what happens if the Site Manager doesn't trust the engineer? The engineer may be a fine upstanding professional – most of them are – but the Site Manager is ultimately responsible for the job and if the engineer or technician hasn't earned his trust yet, it might be wise to check the setting out.

The Site Manager has of course, other options where he doesn't fully trust the site engineer. He could rely on his own judgement, hope for the best – and carry on – comforting himself in the knowledge that, if things do go wrong, at least it wasn't him that hired the engineer. If it all works out well this approach might be ok, however if the building, or some part of it, is set out wrong, there will be no hiding place from responsibility for the Site Manager.

It is all very well checking setting out – but if the Site Manager doesn't know how to do this – then he can't check it, can he?

9.2   Scale

All drawings issued by the architect and consulting engineers, other than sketched details of small objects, are drawn to scale. Common scales used are 1:50, 1:100, 1:500 etc. Lengths are drawn to $1/50^{th}$ of their true length for scales of 1:50; $1/100^{th}$ for scales of 1:100 and so on. Road maps sold in service stations commonly use scales of 1:400,000. Maps issued by the Ordinance Survey of Ireland for use with planning applications etc. are normally to scales of 1:2500 and 1:10560.

The scale used will be indicated on the drawing, and sometimes more than one scale will be used on the one drawing. On the drawing of a house, the plan may be drawn at 1:100 while a detail might be blown up to 1:20.

9.3   The Scale Ruler

A scale ruler is a simple tool to use, and it can be very useful as well as being very dangerous. Scale rulers usually have 7 different scales along with 1:1. Triangular shaped scale rules usually have 10 scales along with 1:1. It is important to ensure that the scale used on the drawing is the one selected on the scale ruler, and this is problem is normally overcome with experience.

When a dimension is not given on a drawing, it is a common practice to measure it with a scale ruler. There are a number of dangers associated with this practise. If the drawing is not an original – it may perhaps be a photocopy, the accuracy of the scale cannot be guaranteed. The photocopier may not represent the scale accurately, resulting in a scale appearing on the photocopied drawing which is in fact incorrect. So if a drawing has to be scaled, it should always be an original. Even with an original scaling is a dangerous practice, if a drawing is in the office for a while it may be affected by dampness and as a result may have changed size – again affecting the accuracy. A change of 2mm (not uncommon in a sheet of paper) will make a dimension alteration of 200 mm if the scale is 1:100. This is a huge variation and proves the dangers associated with scaling from damp drawings.

Where a specific dimension is required and is not on the drawings, it is wise to ask the architect or the consulting engineer for the information, and scaling the drawing should only be done as a last resort.

9.4   Basic Setting Out.

Most setting out is done nowadays with an instrument called a Total Station. These instruments calculate distance and angles electronically and, once you know how to use them, greatly simplify the setting out process. Most Site Managers will not be expected to use these machines, unless, of course, they come from an engineering background. Detailed instructions on the use of Total Stations will not be covered in this book. The Site Manager should, however, be familiar with the broad outline of how they work.

Normally the architect or consulting engineer will furnish the contractor with a drawing showing a reference point, which has a given an address or a reference. This reference may be 0,0 but is more likely to be 100,100.

So what do these numbers mean? It is very simple – these numbers are the Easting and Northing references, and this is the point from which all other measurements are set out on the site. (Note: The Easting is always the first number given except in the

USA and Canada where the Northing is always given first,) So 100,100 simply means 100 metres East and 100 metres North. It should be noted that these references to North and East are not necessarily true North or East. The whole reference system is devised by the land surveyor at the planning stage and simply refers to an invisible grid system designed by the surveyor and imposed on the site plan.

The reason that 100,100 is used instead of 0,0 is that frequently the engineers or technician may need to venture further west or further south than this point, and using 100,100 minimises the need to use negative numbers. Rather than using –3, -45 the same co-ordinates will be 97,55 by using 100,100 as the reference point. (This practice is common too with levels on a site, where a given level, or bench mark, is often called 100, rather than 0.)

Even if he is unable to operate the Total Station, the Site Manager can still check much of the setting out manually – without use of the instrument – if the drawings show two known points, or one known point and one known direction.

9.5   Station Points

What are two known points? If the point 100,100 or other reference point is visible on the site – if it can physically be found on the ground – then this is one known point – called a station point. The Site Manager can't guess which direction is north or east despite how certain he may be. So he needs a second known point, and its reference or address. Then he can calculate distances on the drawings, from these two points, and can measure these distances on the site. However if the second reference point is not available, it may be the case that a direction is known. If the site runs along an existing building line, a wall, or a road, or some similar straight line which will not be disturbed during the construction process, this may be the "known" direction.

So lets say the point he wants to find on the ground has an address of 125,140. We know that the first number 125 is the easting and it will be found 25metres to the east of the reference point 100,100. (25metres being the difference between 125 and 100.) On a similar basis, the 140 refers to 40metres to the North. So the Site Manager can physically go out with his steel tape and find that point on the ground. It's that simple.

The Site Manager should always use a steel tape for checking setting out. Use of any tape that could stretch, or have it's length altered in any way by water or dampness should not be used.

9.6   Grid Lines And Offset Pegs or Profiles

Some drawings show a grid line system. These may be denoted by letters, for lines in one direction, and numbers for the lines at ninety degrees to the others. At the commencement of the works, profiles can be erected by driving wooden pegs or posts along the site perimeter on the grid lines (or a set distance from the grid line.) A string line can be tied between these points to "carry" the line through a certain point, or they can be "sighted." Equally the Site Manager can measure from these profiles to check dimensions. The profiles should be located where they will not be disturbed during the construction process, and in such a way as to prevent movement.

Excavator or other machine drivers working on the site should be instructed to completely destroy the profile posts or pegs – should they accidentally hit them with the machine, or otherwise disturb them. This will prevent the continued use of a profile after it has moved or been re-located by guesswork on the part of the driver. The site engineer can accurately reinstate the profile once it is clear that it has been disturbed.

These profiles can be used by the Site Manager, or indeed anyone else, to check location throughout the construction process.

9.7   Dimensions

It is easy to check dimensions and the Site Manager should do so, frequently. In addition, the Site Manager should perform his checks in full view of the engineer and any trades involved; this will send a signal to them that he is checking their work, and that he makes no apology for doing so.

9.8   Plumb, Level and Angles

Equally, the Site Manager can easily check plumb and level, and again, should carry out these checks in full view of tradesmen and engineers. Angles are relatively straightforward also. In the case of right angles, most people know about the 3,4,5 method of checking. (This is where a triangle is drawn with sides exactly 3, 4 and 5 metres long. If metres will produce a triangle that's too big, you can use feet or whatever unit you like so long as the sides are 3, 4 and 5 units respectively. The angle formed where the lines that are 3 and 4 units long join, will be ninety degrees. This triangle can be marked out and cut from a sheet of plywood, or framed up using suitable timber, and is useful for checking corners.) Some angles, those involving even multiples of 30, 45, 60, and 90 degrees can be worked out easily. Other angles are a bit more difficult and may require the use of a scientific calculator.

Where the Site Manager finds what he believes to be an error, he should invite the Engineer to explain the situation, in an effort to clarify the situation.

Levels will be marked on the drawings as will the master bench mark. Using a dumpy level, it is easy to check levels from the master bench mark. Transferred bench marks are marks, the level of which has been established from the master bench mark. Checking will be made easier if these are in use on the site. Again, transferred bench-marks should be completely destroyed and accurately re-established, if accidentally disturbed.

The practice of checking levels on one floor, from the floor below, is a risky one, as any error in the floor from which the level is taken, will be carried through. This risk is present when any surface other than a bench mark is used as a reference from which to calculate a subsequent level.

9.9   Recording Results Of Checks

A note should be made in the site diary, of the checks carried out and the results achieved. Some indication will need to be included to identify the exact location where the checks were made.

If the firm uses quality control sheets or forms, the record can be made there. The advantage of making the entry in the site diary is that this is retained on site – whereas any record sheets may be returned to head office before completion of the job.

9.10   Dealing With Discrepancies

If the Site Manager uncovers a genuine error, he should immediately make enquiries with the relevant tradesman and the site engineer or technician, to ascertain how the discrepancy occurred. The discrepancy may be small and may have no apparent knock-on effect – the error may be a stand-alone problem. The error may be inside the acceptable tolerances as set out in the specifications. But equally, it could be outside these tolerances, and may have a knock-on impact on other trades or finishes. The Site Manager must satisfy himself fully that the error won't have any knock-on effect and is adequately insignificant before he lets the error go uncorrected. Once an error is discovered or brought to the attention of the Site Manager he becomes complicit in any cover up from the client or head office, or any failure to deal with it, and is just as guilty or perhaps even more so, as the tradesman who made the error in the first place.

The minute an error is discovered or brought to the Site Manager's attention, it should be dealt with there and then. Even seemingly insignificant discrepancies have a nasty habit of coming back to haunt the Site Manager at a later stage.

HALFEN·DEHA

YOUR BEST CONNECTIONS

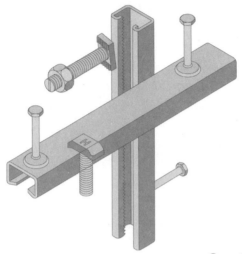

Cast–in channels & T-head Bolts

Halfen Supply a wide range of cast-in channels and T-head bolts for vibration and dust free fixings to concrete.

Applications include masonry and cladding support, curtain-walling, canopies and balustrades.

For the full range contact

Construction Accessories Ltd
Toughers Industrial Estate
Newhall, Naas,
Co. Kildare
Tel: 045-438691 Fax 045-438690
www.constructionaccessories.ie

Chapter 10 – HEALTH & SAFETY AND THE SITE MANAGER

10.1   Introduction

This book does not attempt to address all of the various safety issues on construction sites. These are too varied and too numerous to be dealt with here. Nor is it a safety manual. What is attempted is, to give the Site Manager in insight to some of the issues he will come across, and provide a resource to point him in the direction of increased site safety.

10.2   The Health & Safety Authority (HSA)

The Health and Safety Authority (HSA) is the national body in Ireland with responsibility for securing health and safety at work. It is a state-sponsored body, operating under the Safety, Health and Welfare at Work Act, 2005 and it reports to the Minister for Enterprise, Trade and Employment. The Authority consults widely with employers, employees and their respective organisations. To help develop sound policies and good workplace practices, the Authority works with various Advisory Committees and Task Forces etc. which focus on specific occupations and hazards.

10.3   Fatalities

Much has been spoken and written about Health & Safety in the construction industry. The HSA has published numerous relevant documents, and the Construction Industry Federation (CIF) has issued many guidelines for sites on the topic. In addition, each main contractor has his Health & Safety Plan, as has each sub-contractor on the site, or at least he should have, and many have dedicated Safety Officers.

So with all this documentation and policy in place, how do so many accidents occur in construction, and why do an average of nineteen workers get killed on sites in Ireland each year?

Many Site Managers complain that while Head Office talks a lot about Health & Safety, in reality insufficient time and resources are provided to carry out site tasks in a completely safe manner. Many say Health & Safety is delegated completely to site; the attitude of Head Office being "Health & Safety is an operational matter." In addition, the HSA has inadequate resources to police the sites, and apart from much pre-publicised blitzes – contractors know that visits from the authorities are few and far between. Many construction firms behave in the belief that if you take a safety risk on site, the chances of going undetected would appear to be good.

A report prepared for the Health & Safety Authority in December 2003 by Marie Dalton B.A. M.Sc. of the Centre for Civil and Construction Engineering at The University of Manchester Institute of Science and Technology makes interesting reading. While I do not like to selectively quote from any published work for fear of misrepresenting what is stated, this report clearly states: "...unless safety is given priority at board level, it is most unlikely that time or resources will be available for effective safety performance at the operational level." (–Page 13.) Dalton goes on to state that 425 inspections of construction sites took place in June and September of 2003 as part of the European Construction Campaign and that written or verbal warnings were issued on 78% of visits, formal improvement notices were served during 7% of visits with 15% of visits resulting in the cessation of work. (–Page 15.)

Designers were severely criticised by Dalton also. "..the majority of designers were unaware of the General Principle of Prevention under the Regulations, let alone its content or implications. Only 10% of designers have any health and safety qualification.... Inspectors report that decisions by designers have produced site conditions that were so dangerous as to require immediate cessation of work." (–Page 17.) Prosecution against designers is almost unheard of in Ireland.

Widespread dissatisfaction in the UK with the Construction (Design and Management) Regulations (CDM) 1994 has prompted a review and *The Strategic Forum for Construction* chaired by Sir John Egan makes a very interesting proposal. "All members of the project, including specialist contractors should be appointed before the design stage. The theory is that each interested party would be consulted on the parts of the design that affected them, that responsibility for risk would be shared and so risk could be designed out before construction begins." (–Broughton 2001.) Dalton correctly notes that several of the proposed amendments to the UK legislation are relevant to Irish legislation also, this being a good example.

Table 1	
Fatalities on Irish Construction Sites 1997 – 2005	
Source H.S.A	
1997	15
1998	22
1999	18
2000	17
2001	22
2002	21
2003	20
2004	16
2005	23

If all of the guidelines issued by the various bodies *"up the line"* were followed, there is no doubt that accidents on sites would be greatly minimized, and fatalities would be extremely rare. But we don't live or work in an ideal world.

Health and Safety like all other issues must be "managed" on site, and this is the Site Managers role. It is vital that the Site Manager takes a firm leadership role on safety matters. Dangerous work practices must be stopped the minute they are detected, and disciplinary action must be taken with offenders. The type of action taken may vary from a "telling-off" to dismissal – depending on the seriousness of the offence and the style of the Site Manger – but action *must* be taken. Failure to act in the face of serious safety risks is tantamount to endorsement of the dangerous work practices themselves and sets a dangerous precedent; one that will almost certainly come back to haunt the Site Manager and may add to the fatality statistics in the industry.

The Site Manager must not let the pressures exerted by head office for speed of construction compromise his demands for safe work practices. When the Contracts Manager, Contracts Director and/or Managing Director visit the site, irrespective of how loud they may be in their condemnation of progress, the Site Manager should clearly and unapologetically state the reasons for delay. After all their tune would be different if someone had been killed on the site as a direct result of safety inadequacies in a "push" to meet deadlines.

Of course, the Site Manager cannot cite "safety concerns" as an excuse for (his own) poor management of resources. The delegation from head office will soon see through this, and as result, may not listen to the Site Managers genuine concerns later, a bit like the "boy who cried wolf."

10.4   Safety Issues To Be Addressed By The Site Manager.

The following as a non-exhaustive list of particular risks to the safety and health of persons at work:

- *Work which puts persons at work at risk of burial under earth falls, engulfment in swampland or falling from a height, where the risk is particularly aggravated by the nature of the work or processes used or by the environment at the place of work or site.*
- *Work which puts persons at work at risk from chemical or biological substances constituting a particular danger to the safety and health of such persons or involving a legal requirement for health monitoring.*
- *Work with ionising radiation requiring the designation of controlled or supervised areas.*
- *Work near high voltage power lines.*
- *Work exposing persons at work to the risk of drowning.*
- *Work on wells, underground earthworks and tunnels.*
- *Work carried out by divers at work having a system of air supply.*

- *Work carried out in a caisson with a compressed-air atmosphere.*
- *Work involving the use of explosives.*
- *Work involving the assembly or dismantling of heavy prefabricated components.*

Indeed, the issues facing the Site Manager in his efforts to maintain a safe place for workers and visitors are many and varied. On the assumption that people cause most accidents we will commence with the people that the Site Manager will come in direct contact with during the course of his work.

10.4.1 Direct Employees

Operatives and Trades people directly employed by the main contractor will normally not challenge the Site Manager's authority to any great extent, in matters of site-safety. They are paid for their time and as such will normally do what is asked of them. Good clear communication of instructions (Chapter 7) is, however, essential. The Site Manager must outline what is expected and the minimum standard that is acceptable. Safety should be a collective issue, and sometimes asking direct employees for their help in maintaining a safe site, can be more effective than issuing threats.

Site Engineers and other Professional and Administrative personnel should in theory help the Site Manager to achieve a safe site. He needs to explain to them what his objectives are, and again ask for their help. Some Site Engineers don't see safety issues as their concern at all, not realising that safety is everybody's responsibility on the site.

10.4.2 Agency Labour.

Agency Labourers, like direct-employees are paid on a time basis, so they will have no problem following the Site Mangers instructions. But because they may not have been on the site all along, they may be unaware of their duties in respect of safety. While the Site Induction covers this, it is important that the Site Managers expectation is clearly communicated – he can't assume that the Agency Labourer will know what is expected, himself. After all he may have come from a site where the standards are much lower, or maybe from a non-construction background.

10.4.3 Sub Contractors & Their Employees

Sub Contactors are a major worry for the Site Manager from a Health and Safety point of view. They normally have taken work on a price, and their priorities usually centre on productivity. Some sub-contractors have progressed to the self-employed level without any safety training other than Safe Pass. The sub contractor normally wants to get in, do the job, get paid and move on. While there is nothing at all wrong with that in principle, there may be much wrong with the way that he goes about doing the job from a safety point of view.

Common shortcuts taken include,

- Inadequate or no PPE,
- Unauthorised alteration or removal of scaffolding,
- Inadequate protection of their own work (e.g. groundworkers leaving excavations unprotected)
- Overloading (block-layers/bricklayers overloading scaffolds, or roofers overloading roof sections which could collapse under the weight causing serious injury or death.)

The potential problems seem almost endless.

Employees of sub-contractors are often sent to site without proper materials, tools and equipment, and frequently, without proper supervision. Sub Contractors are discussed in detail in Chapter 8.

10.4.4 Visitors

The term *Visitors* includes the Design Team, Client, Head Office Representatives, Approved visitors to the site and Trespassers. The Site Manager must insist on all visitors to the site wearing appropriate PPE. It is amazing how many Managing Directors of construction companies will go to site and have a "walk-about" without wearing appropriate PPE. They may not have appropriate footwear or may not wear a hard hat. While the Site Manager should not embarrass the MD by publicly reminding him of the Safety Rules on site, a quite word in private should be said. Managing Directors are not exempt from the rules either.

10.4.5 The Design Team

Members of the Design Team are frequent offenders when it comes to PPE. Again a quiet word is the most appropriate method of dealing with the problem. I don't believe it should be raised at site meetings, a result of which could be an entry in the minutes and there is nothing to be gained by embarrassing members of the design team in this manner.

10.4.6 The Client

The Client may be major offender when it comes to wearing PPE on site visits. Often the client will have no experience of construction and should be accompanied at all times on site visits. He may be totally unaware of the dangers posed on sites, and breaches of site rules may extend well beyond the failure to wear PPE. Great care has to be taken when the client visits the site, and it is often advantageous for the Site Manager to personally accompany the client on the "walk-about." The Site Manager may get an insight into the way the client is thinking about the project and may be able to anticipate problems or issues that may arise later at site meetings, as a result of the joint "walk-about." One point to remember is that the Site Manager should not let the Client get a reciprocal insight into the way he is thinking, and shouldn't be caught on the hop with questions he may not want to answer at that particular time.

10.4.7   Sales Reps And Delivery Drivers

Visiting sales representatives and delivery drivers, will call to the site from time to time and while these individuals are normally well trained in on-site behaviour, their presence cannot go unchecked. Depending on the size of the firm or the size of the site, the culture of the firm, or the Site Manager's approach, there may or may not be a signing-in procedure to be followed. Irrespective of the procedures in place, the Site Manager can't let the visitor be the victim of, or the cause of, an accident or incident. Vigilance is again called for, and the visitor should certainly not be allowed the freedom to wander around the site. A small area should be provided where visitors can sit and wait while their host is summoned.

10.4.8   Other Visitors

Other visitors may call from time to time and the purpose of their visit should be clearly established. Perhaps they are checking out security or storage of tools and materials for a future raid. Irrespective of their motivation for visiting, they should be stopped at the gate and interviewed, and procedures should be in place to prevent their entry beyond that point, unless invited.

10.4.9   Trespassers

Trespassers are a major worry for every business in every industry. The Site Manager must ensure (by delegation,) that the site is left as safe as possible overnight and at weekends. Openings in floors and ceilings should be securely sealed and/or cordoned off immediately. Signage should be used extensively. Great care should be taken in the way that materials are stored. Heavy items, which, if they fell, could seriously injure someone, should be secured in a manner that will minimise the chances of such a fall. While the Site Manager won't be able to prevent every possible injury to trespassers, it is his duty to take all reasonable and practical steps. No comfort can be taken from the fact that the visitor was a trespasser, if any injury occurs, and the nuisance value alone of justifying the storage procedures in place, with all it's resultant paper work and lost time, should be a sufficient deterrent to the Site Manager, from careless housekeeping.

10.5   Other Challenges.

Of course there are many health & safety concerns other than the people related ones listed above. Issues relating to materials, equipment, paper work and training are all relevant.

10.5.1 Plant & Equipment.

The use of plant & equipment on site is another issue needing both a definite policy and vigilance. Operatives of certain power tools should wear additional PPE. Concrete cutting saws (con-saws) and angle grinders are two that spring to mind. Both are used for cutting steel and operatives should wear safety goggles or similar eye-protection while using these tools.

Some suppliers of cartridge operate tools and fixings have qualified personnel to give short training programmes on the use of this equipment. This training usually takes forty-five minutes to an hour and it is well worthwhile, and is normally provided free of charge. If the Site Manager decides to bring in this type of trainer, he should have a simple form prepared for the operatives to sign, stating that they have received the training, and these forms should be filed away in the office. They can be produced at a Health & Safety inspection as proof that you are proactive in training.

10.5.2 Machinery.

Machines on site should of course be in good working order. This includes telescopic forklifts, excavators of all types and sizes, dumpers, rollers, cranes, lorries, graders etc. The Site Manager should visually check these machines at least once a week for excessive wear in pins, oil leaks, lighting and the like. He cannot be expected to conduct a thorough safety check on the machine, but the results of his visual inspection should be recorded in the Site Diary. Needless to say, deficiencies noticed, should be brought to the attention of the plant manager or relevant sub-contractor, and the machine should not be used until it has been repaired or replaced. Certificates for the various machines on site should be filed away in the site office, as should copies of the Drivers' Construction Skills Card. Only drivers with appropriate certificates should be permitted to drive machines on site. (See 10.7.19)

10.5.3 Fire Extinguishers.

Suitable Fire Extinguishers should be maintained on site and located where they can easily be accessed if required. Appropriate signage should be used to indicate their location and suitability. The suitability issue is a big one, as some fire extinguishers are unsuitable for certain types of fire. All personnel should be trained in the use of the equipment. Suppliers may be willing to provide some basic training and this should be availed of, with participants signing the form to confirm their attendance at the training. Again this should be filed away safely.

10.5.4 Risk Assessments & Method Statements.

Method Statements for specific tasks to be performed on site should be on file. The Method Statement is just that – a statement of the method to be used to safely carry out the specific task. Method statements can, and should, only be drafted after a risk assessment has taken place.

Risk assessments are relatively simple to carryout. It boils down to:

- What are the risks? (Identification of the risks.)
- Who is at risk? (Further identification of the risks.)
- What can be done to minimise the risks? (Looking at the various options)
- Who will be responsible? (Taking action)

Many sub-contractors will have method statements included as part of their safety documentation presented to site before they commence work. The method statements should be checked thoroughly as they frequently consist of general and almost meaningless words placed strategically to make a page look full. How can exactly the same risks apply on each site? As stated above, the method can only be decided after the specific risks are assessed.

Specialist suppliers to the site may also be willing to give a short presentation on installation of their products. One such product that comes to mind is timber-frame house kits. While these are relatively straightforward, any specific hazards which installation or erection of the kit may produce, should be discussed with the kit-erectors and operatives working nearby. Some will claim that is an issue strictly for the Risk Assessment and Method Statement, but the presentation will aid communication to workers on the safety aspect of the job.

10.5.5   Storage and Use of Hazardous Chemicals And Materials

Many products used in construction processes are quite hazardous if used improperly. Product data sheets and product safety sheets are normally available from the manufacturers and/or suppliers of these products. These should be consulted before the materials are used, and particular note should be taken of any additional PPE requirements. Storage of materials has safety, as well as security, implications. Great care has to be taken with poisonous and toxic substances – to prevent accidents while the site is open and when trespassers may call. Again, as with other safety risks on the site, little comfort can be drawn from the fact that the victim was an intruder, if an accident occurs.

10.5.6   PPE Book

All PPE issued should be recorded in a PPE Book, where the recipient signs for what he received and when. This keeps track of the physical stock, acts as proof that the Site Manager is doing his job, and reinforces the case for disciplinary action, should operatives fail to observe the PPE rules on site. The Site Manager, of course, has to ensure that sufficient supplies are stocked – or the whole PPE issue will become farcical.

10.5.7   Safety Representative.

Any site where there are more than twenty workers must have a Safety Representative. The workers on that site select the Safety Representative, to represent them on issues related to Safety, Health and Welfare in the place of work. If the workforce goes over twenty, say unexpectedly, the Site Manager could nominate a Safety Representative, to act until such time as the selection process takes place. The Site Manager should however put the onus on the workers to select their Safety Representative. The name of the nominated or selected representative should be recorded in the site diary, and should be updated as changes take place.

The selection of Safety Representative is a critical appointment. The Site Manager should work closely with the Safety Representative, involving him in key decisions and working with him rather than ignoring them or treating him as a spy or as some sort of a nuisance.

The Site Manager must take into account concerns expressed by the Safety Representative, and must inform him when an Inspector from the HSA calls. The role is one of a "middle-man" between site management and the workforce, and the Site Manager should enlist his help to make the site safer.

10.6   Site Inductions.

Before the days of the Fás Safe Pass, Site Inductions were the main source of safety training for many people engaged in the construction industry. Just because the Fás Safe Pass Certification system is in place now, Site Managers should not ignore the Site Induction. This is a very useful opportunity to get to know new operatives on the site and explain how you want things done. Many companies have their own list of topics for inclusion in the Site Induction, and the Construction Industry Federation has published a useful booklet offering guidance also.

The following is a suggested agenda for the Site Induction. It is not by any means intended as an exhaustive list, and the manner in which each Site Manager approaches the Induction and the priority he gives to each topic will be a matter of personal choice drawn perhaps, from experience. Initial reaction may well be: "Twenty Items – That'll take all day" or: "I haven't time for all that."

Indeed some Site Mangers are reluctant to stand up in front of a number of people and give a structured presentation. They may find it difficult addressing people that they know. It's a leadership issue and a management function. It has to be dealt with. The only other alternative is the weapon of mass delegation. If the Site Manager can't or won't do the presentation himself, it is important that there is somebody else on the site trained to carry out the inductions and that the presentation will follow along the same lines. While delegation of the task is fine, delegation of the responsibility is not an option. Make sure that Site Inductions are carried out, and carried out to an acceptable standard. Every operative who will be working on the site should be inducted into the safety-training programme. There should be no exceptions.

Whilst giving the presentation, it may help to have a few notes written on a card, within easy reading distance. Prompt-points to prevent accidental omissions. Eye contact with the people on the programme should be maintained – this is very important.

Many points will take a very short time to present. The first four points can be dealt with in a few sentences.

The following is a suggested list with notes immediately following.

10.7　　The Site Induction Agenda

1　　　　Welcome To The Site
2　　　　Induction Objectives
3　　　　Safety Objectives
4　　　　Project Details
5　　　　Main Causes of Accidents
6　　　　Management Structure
7　　　　Safety Representative
8　　　　Site Layout
9　　　　The Site Rules

10   Company Responsibilities
11   Your Responsibilities
12   Specific Hazards / Safe System Of Work Plan
13   PPE
14   Accident Reporting Procedures
15   First Aid
16   Emergency Procedures
17   Communications
18   FÁS Safe Pass
19   Constructions Skills Certificates
20   Questions & Answers

10.7.1 Welcome To The Site

This only takes a few words: "Hello. My name is... and you're all very welcome to the site" or something along those lines. If you are comfortable with the idea, you could shake hands with each of the people present for the induction, but it's not necessary.

10.7.2 Induction Objectives

Careful here. The speaker has to be clear in his own mind what the objectives of the induction are. If the motivation for giving the induction presentation is solely to "go through the motions" or "be seen to be doing something" then a major problem exists and the presentation should be cancelled. The speaker has to believe in the idea – in the concept, and his motivation for giving the presentation must be genuine, otherwise, the workers will see through him, the safety culture on the site will be flawed, and it is almost certain that there will be a number of accidents on the site. The objectives should be to inform the workers of the site safety rules, to explain exactly what is to be built, the risks associated with the project, and to ensure that a safe working environment is in place.

10.7.3 Safety Objectives

The objectives should be to get the project built safely with no accidents and to make every worker on the site, more safety conscious.

10.7.4 Project Details

This is where the speaker tells the audience what exactly is to be built and the expected completion date. You would be surprised how many workers arrive on site without a clue as to what the job is about, or the work involved.

10.7.5 Main Causes of Accidents

This section of the presentation serves to remind everyone that the major causes of accidents are falling from heights or objects falling on to people.
- 43% of all fatalities on Irish sites are due to falls from heights.
- 43% of construction fatalities were General Operatives.
- 46% of fatalities from 1997-2002 occurred on sites with five workers or less.

10.7.6 Management Structure

Explain the management structure of the company. Identify the director or senior manager responsible for health and safety in the organisation.

10.7.7 Safety Representative

The name of the Safety Representative should be clearly posted for all workers and visitors to the site to see. The safety representative should be introduced to each new worker as he comes to the site, ideally at the induction.

10.7.8 Site Layout

The site layout may be very obvious with hoarding or fencing clearly defining the boundaries and good signage indicating where the canteen, toilets, stores etc are. But a quick run-through everything won't do any harm and won't take too long.

10.7.9 The Site Rules

This is an important one and needs attention. What are the site rules? Make sure these are written out before the presentation commences – it's no good making them up as you go along.

These may include:
- Operate in a safe manner at all times
- PPE (discussed later)
- Working Hours
- Work permits for certain tasks?
- On site speed limits.
- Use of mobile phones while operating certain plant and equipment.

as well as other rules.

10.7.10 Company Responsibilities

The Company responsibilities should be clearly set out in the Safety Statement and should be included in the presentation.

10.7.11 Your Responsibilities

In this section the presenter should outline the responsibilities of the workers on the site in terms of health & safety. Again this should be taken from the company's Safety Statement.

10.7.12 Specific Hazards / Safe System OF Work Plan (SSWP)

What are the specific hazards on this site? Perhaps the

project involves working at heights, within confined spaces, with dangerous chemicals or involves other dangerous work practices. Are there risks entering and leaving the site from traffic on the main road or access roads? Are there any overhead power lines running across the site?

Whatever risks are specific to this site need to be identified, listed, and gone through in the presentation. The presenter should bear in mind that specific risks change with the building process. At the commencement of the job, there may be no risk associated with working at heights, but as the building progresses, this might become a real risk. This presents two issues for the Induction process: How the risks are to be addressed in the induction presentation, and how to make remote (in terms of time) risks seem real and relevant.

The danger of not including remote risks in the presentations at the commencement of the job, is that workers who are inducted at the commencement and remain on the site all through, are not properly inducted as the new risks develop.

The presenter needs to visualise the entire job through before any inductions are carried out, and if new specific risks develop during the job, he should ensure that all workers on the site are made aware of these new risks in an additional presentation.

Safe System Of Work Plans are available from the H.S.A. These forms cover various site activities. The Site Manager should insist that these are completed before the various specific tasks are undertaken and that all parties involved in the process sign the form.

10.7.13 PPE

What are the rules on your site regarding the use of Personal Protective Equipment? How strictly are they going to be observed? The use of PPE is one of the key issues on every site. The Site Manager should state his policy clearly.

(The Site Manager needs to ensure that adequate stocks of hard hats, gloves, dust masks, eye and ear protection etc is readily available, as stated in 10.5.6.)

In addition to the normal PPE items, protective overalls or aprons may be needed when using certain chemicals.

10.7.14 Accident Reporting Procedures

It is important to have a clear policy in relation to the reporting of accidents and reportable incidents – also know as "near misses." If an accident occurs the Site Manager needs to know about it, and needs to know about it quickly. So the procedure for reporting accidents should be clearly stated at the induction presentation. Reporting procedure should be simple to implement – if it is unnecessarily difficult it just won't be carried out. The Site Manager should write the accident into the Accident Book when he has an accurate comprehension of exactly what occurred. In the case of serious injuries, the Site Manager may have to compile an accident report. This topic is dealt with in Chapter 2.

10.7.15 First Aid

The location of the first aid kit should be clearly indicated to everyone on site and the induction is the place to do it. Equally the identification of the trained first-aider should be communicated to the workers. (The contents of he first aid kit should be checked frequently and stocked up as necessary.)

A list of local medical practitioners with their telephone numbers should be displayed clearly in a number of places on the site. The opening times of the surgery should be noted on this list if possible.

(It is a good idea to physically check out the location of the nearest hospital with Accident & Emergency facilities before the project commences, so that clear directions can be given in the case of an emergency.)

10.7.16 Emergency Procedures

All operatives should be aware of the emergency procedures on site. The Assembly points should be clearly established, and marked with signage. These points should be kept clear from obstruction at all times. As the project develops these points may need to be changed.

10.7.17 Communications

Communications on-site is a much more relevant issue nowadays with he influx of non-Irish national workers into this country. Interpreters may be required for some workers, particularly during the site induction, or for other training meetings. The Site Manager should satisfy himself that each worker understands all of the aspects of the site induction. This is a very important point, and implementation of it may be a nuisance, but what is the point in bringing people to a training session if they don't understand the language? If they don't know what is being said, do you really think that they will observe all the safety requirements? Many non-Irish nationals work in groups or gangs and usually have someone in their group who can translate for the others.

10.7.18 FÁS Safe Pass

It is a requirement that all workers on sites in Ireland have a current FÁS Safe Pass Certificate. These should be checked before the end of the induction and the details should be recorded on a register and kept in the site office.

10.7.19 Constructions Skills Certificates

Construction Skills Certificates, issued by FÁS, are required for certain jobs on site, including tractor/dozer operation, mobile crane operation, crawler crane operation, articulated dumper operation, site dumper operation, 180° excavator operation, 360° excavator operation, roof and wall cladding sheeting, built up roof felting and of course scaffolding.

Copies of the certificates should be filed in the site office, or a register maintained, recording the name of the holder, tasks covered by the certificate, the expiry date and the number of the certificate. The Site Manager should periodically conduct spot checks on the site for appropriate certificates and record the findings in the site diary. (A list of workers who require CSCS cards appears in Schedule 4 at the end of this book.)

10.7.20 Questions & Answers

Before the Induction Presentation is completed operatives should be invited to ask any questions and these should be dealt with thoroughly and sincerely.

It is important that each person inducted, signs the relevant form and those these are collected and maintained in the site office.

10.8 Where should the induction take place?

The induction presentation should be held in the meeting room or somewhere where there will be the minimum of disruptions.

10.9 When should inductions be held?

Every worker should be inducted prior to commencement of work on the site. One option is to ask each sub-contractor appointed to bring in all of the operatives that he expects to deploy on the site, for one Induction session. This will minimise the need for Site Inductions taking place almost daily.

10.10 Tool Box Talks.

Toolbox talks are short safety presentations usually held in the canteen at break time. They normally cover one specific topic and are reminders of the need to be safety conscious on site at all times. A list of 50 potential topics is included in Schedule 5 at the rear of this book. The list is presented in no specific order, and Site Managers might want to select the talks in the same order as the work progresses on the site. I always recommend that operatives attending the talk should sign an attendance register, which is filed away in the site office.

10.11 Don't Take Chances

Irrespective of the pressure applied, the Site Manager should never put the lives of his fellow workers on the site at risk. Everyone has the right to return from work safely. A delay of a day here and there to provide proper safe facilities is very little when you think of the life of a building.

Never send a co-worker to his death on site.

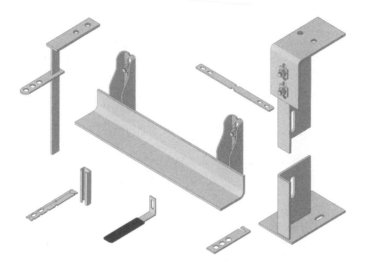

Brickwork Support, Ties & Windposts

Halfen supply a wide range of brickwork support and restraint products, either off-the-shelf or bespoke.

For the full range contact

Chapter 11 – QUALITY MANAGEMENT ON SITE

11.1   Quality Policy

Quality is not just a site issue and, like safety, is much talked about in the industry.

While some companies operate an ISO or similar quality system, the majority do not. Many firms operate on the minimalist basis – preferring the very least standard that can be gotten away with.   Yet no Managing Director when talking to architects or potential clients will ever say: "Give me that job so that I can make a mess of it, cut every corner and break your heart in the process." This is equally true of the sub contractor calling to your site, looking for an opportunity to quote for part of the job. Everybody talks the quality talk.

The various stages of construction can be broken down into two categories for discussion purposes on quality: Structural work and Finishes.   In structural matters quality can affect the integrity of the building, while quality of finishes is important to avoid expensive and time-consuming snagging.

But first we will ask the question: what exactly is quality?

There are many definitions of quality but the one I prefer is:

The measurement of performance against expectation.

This is a great definition of quality from a construction perspective. *If it meets expectation*.   Expectation may be as documented in detail in the specifications or maybe as simple as satisfying a visual examination.

It is unfortunate that quality is nearly always left to the Site Manager to deliver.   Quality should be designed into the job; it should be taken into account when choosing suppliers and sub contractors, and when selecting materials. It is very difficult for the Site Manager to deliver a quality project, if the quality ethic begins and ends at the site gate.   Nevertheless, it is his job and he has to deliver the very best quality that he can.

If he is to deliver quality, the Site Manager should liaise with the Purchasing Manager, the Quantity Surveyor, the Contracts Manager, and the Director in charge of the project (the Managing Director – if necessary) at the start of the job. He should investigate what resources have been provided-for in the tendering process.

11.2 Structural

Whilst most contractors and most site managers pay a lot of attention to structural matters, there are those who, unfortunately, do not. The structural integrity of a building cannot be compromised irrespective of programme deadlines and <u>the Site Manager must resist pressure from head office to speed-up work at the expense of quality</u>. An extra day or two spent ensuring that certain structural matters are fully attended to, will cost a lot less than demolition and re-establishment, later. This is one of the key areas where the Site Manager has to stand up and be counted, often in the face of criticism and even abuse, from his superiors.

The Site Manager must ensure proper supervision and checking of all works which will be permanently covered up, or works of structural significance. He must call an immediate halt to works which are unsatisfactory, and must be fit to withstand the likely abuse he may be subjected to, especially from disgruntled sub-contractors. He must have the mental strength to order the demolition of work which he deems unsatisfactory, and should not lose his temper in the process despite similar emotional reactions from those around him at the time. It is always better to get it right even at a second attempt than let poor workmanship go ahead.

11.3 Finishes.

If *structural* is the unseen, *finishes* are the seen. It is very easy to criticise, and some Managing Directors and Contracts Managers only ever seem to criticise finishes to the Site Manager. They never seem to notice what he got right, only what is not up to standard. This is one of the difficulties of site management and one that takes a lot of getting used to. No Site Manager sets out to deliver poor finishes, but Murphy's Law seems to apply with uncomfortable regularity. It always seems to be the morning when the Site Meeting is due to take place that the carpenter cuts the skirting too short, or the painter dabs the untreated oak door with magnolia emulsion, or the electrician suddenly decides that the finished wall needs another cable run and chasing is well underway when the Site Manager brings the design team on "walk-about." All part of the joys of site management.

There are several preventative measures that the site manager can take with regard to quality of finishes. In the case of Sub Contractors the first place to start is the Pre-Appointment meeting (Chapter 8.) In all cases the Site Manager should explain the standard that he requires and also the standard that he won't tolerate. He should explain the procedures for remedial works. If the electrician suddenly discovers that he needs to run in a new cable in an otherwise finished room, he should be encouraged to come and talk to the Site Manager before he commences work. Then they can collectively agree a timescale that will minimise embarrassment for the Site Manager and a telling-off for the electrician. In return the Site Manager should respect the fact the electrician came to him before destruction commenced, and while he should mark the electrician's card for the original omission, he should not go so far overboard as to deter the electrician from making a voluntary disclosure in the future, should a similar omission recur.

Like structural matters, where problems are discovered they must be dealt with immediately rather than letting poor workmanship go ahead. <u>Poor finishes by one trade, bring down the overall finish of the project for all.</u>

11.4 The Delivery Inspection.

Materials should be inspected upon delivery to site. Their suitability should be considered. If the material delivered varies in any way from what was expected – action needs to be taken immediately. Sometimes the supplier will have substituted one brand for another, often without consultation. Perhaps the purchasing department got it wrong, or maybe the delivery driver has dropped off the wrong consignment from his truck. Whatever the cause, there is no point in waiting until the goods are to be used before making the startling discovery of their unsuitability. There is a risk that if the materials are broadly similar, that they "will have to do now," and as a result quality may be seriously compromised. Defective or otherwise unsuitable materials should not be used.

11.5   Storage & Handling

Storage of materials can greatly affect their individual quality and performance, and that of the overall project. The Site Manager should ensure that:

- There is adequate storage for materials,
- The storage provided is suitable for the material to be stored,
- The materials are handled with sufficient care,
- The materials are handled and stored safely.

Certain materials may be susceptible to dampness or rain and others may have to be stored in a particular way due to their nature or to packaging considerations. The labelling will indicate the storage requirements and these should be followed as closely as possible. While all of this may sound very basic it can be overlooked, and the Site Manager should have a policy in place, and check that those responsible are carrying out that policy.

11.6   Protection of Work

Protection of work has a big bearing on quality. Deficiencies are more conspicuous where finishes are concerned – most people will notice mortar stains on lead flashing and on slates, and damage to finished doors and window boards etc. But less obvious protection may be needed for structural elements of the work. Concrete freshly placed in foundations or decks etc. may need covering or treatment to prevent rapid curing, which may cause cracking, etc.

Protection of work falls into two categories when it comes to workers on site – protection of the work that is being undertaken and protection of existing work from the works which follow-on.

The Site Manager needs to be aware of the potential areas where damage may occur and have a preventative plan and any relevant materials to implement it, in place. He needs to check while the works are in progress that there is no damage to existing works, and he must assess the risk of the occurrence of such damage.

11.7   Covered-up work

It is always tempting to get work covered up quickly especially reinforcement in concrete, wall cavities, and certain roof works. The belief being that when the engineers check out the work, the cover-up limits what they can see and in turn perhaps, complain about. This is fine so long as everything is done to the proper standard. The Site Manager should never cut corners because the opportunity presents itself, and should pride himself in the quality of his work at all times. Rapid covering-up of work can arouse suspicions in engineers – which can have a knock on effect for the Site Manager.

There are, of course, genuine reasons for covering up some works rapidly. Fears concerning the rusting of reinforcing, is a genuine reason for getting the concrete poured quickly. As is the risk of debris or soil falling into the excavations where the concrete is to be poured. There may also be Health & Safety issues concerning open excavations. Untreated timbers in roof construction or the general weathering of the building can be genuine reasons for get on with it as well.

The Site Manager can have a clear conscience after getting work covered up quickly, but engineers do like to see the work before it is covered up, and liaison with the engineers is important to prevent a row later. The Site Manager should also keep a photographic record of the works – in case the row does break out.

11.8   Record Keeping

The goods inwards documentation described in Chapter 2 will track the materials from a purchasing and programme point of view but will not record testing or suitability inspections. There are other records which can help the delivery of quality:

- Record of Slump Tests taken on Concrete when it arrives on site.
- Register of Concrete Cubes formed, listing date, delivery docket number, and exact location of where the concrete was placed.
- Inspection sheets for block work, brickwork, formwork, reinforcement, tanking or other damp proofing and other works.
- Materials Data Sheets
- Photographs

The Site Manager should involve the site engineer in the testing process at all times. It should be a team effort. The Site Manager should also cross check the work of the engineer, and satisfy himself that proper records are kept on site of all the testing which has taken place.

11.9   Responsibility For Quality

Ultimately it is the Site Manager who delivers quality on site. If he is not committed to the quality ethic, standards will slip and a poor quality building or project will be delivered to the client and ultimately the end user. None of us likes poor quality, site managers included. While I said at the outset of this chapter that quality isn't just a site issue, quality performance management *is* a site issue and it is up to the Site Manager to ensure that the quality delivered is the best possible at all times. While a sense of fair play with all trades should be maintained, the Site Manger should instantly and publicly order work to be re-done or made good when he is not satisfied with the quality delivered. The earlier this can be done the better, as it will serve to highlight the standard the Site Manger expects and that which he will not tolerate.

Precast Accessories

Construction Accessories are the leading supplier of accessories to the precast industry. We also support the use of precast units on site.

Levelling shims for accurate positioning of precast units. Available in a range of thicknesses.

Specialist Lifting & Fixing Systems

For safe lifting of precast units into position, we offer a number of solutions in conjunction with the precast provider.
Test certs provided with all lifting attachments.

Construction Accessories Ltd
Toughers Industrial Estate
Newhall, Naas,
Co. Kildare
Tel: 045-438691 Fax 045-438690
www.constructionaccessories.ie

Chapter 12 – CAREER MANAGEMENT

12.1   Time to move on or move up?

Many Site Managers are quite happy in their work, and with their employers. But what happens if the Site Manager is unhappy, gets itchy feet or is unexpectedly headhunted? Maybe he wants to become a Contracts Manager with his existing employers or a new firm.

Somewhere along the line the Site Manager may feel it is time to move on. Many little things may have happened to upset him, and over time they will have combined to become one huge issue or disappointment. Or the Site Manager will feel he has gone as far as he can within a particular organisation and still has ambitions. New personnel may have joined the firm – a Contracts Manager he can't work with, or some member of the family of the firm's founder. Or some other event or set of circumstances may conspire to de-motivate the Site Manager.

Whatever the trigger, the Site Manager will know when it is time to start looking around.

There are a few questions the Site Manager should ask himself before finally deciding to move on.

- Are things as bad here as I think?
  - o Sometimes things are different than they seem. Maybe it's not all that bad after all.
- What are the good points of the present situation?
  - o It is helpful to write these down on a sheet of paper. Every job has good points no matter how bad the job is.
  - o Is it worth risking these for a change?
- What are the bad points?
  - o Once these are written down they may seem smaller than first thought – or they may be much bigger.
  - o Maybe it is just a phase the firm is going through. Perhaps the problems are on a different site and the firm is under pressure as a result.

- o Maybe the firm hasn't a lot of work on, and head office behaviour will return to normal once they pick up a new job.
- Perhaps it's not a company problem?
  - o Maybe it is the Site Manager himself that has changed. Is this project getting to him? The next one will probably be better.
  - o Maybe it is his health or the travelling or traffic-congestion related to this job.
  - o Maybe there is family pressure on the Site Manager.
- Will it blow over?
  - o It is possible that things will revert to normal.
  - o The crisis may blow over and any decision to up and go will be hasty.
- If it was better before what has changed?
  - o What *exactly* has changed?
- Are the problems real or imaginary?
  - o Is it a physical problem – can it be clearly identified? Maybe it is a *perceived* problem.
- Would it be any different elsewhere?
  - o Maybe the problem is industry wide.
- Would changing jobs now make any real difference?
  - o Maybe other firms are going through a similar phase to the one his current employers are going through.
- What have I got to lose if I go?
  - o Where am I located within the structure of the firm here? If I leave I will be "last-in" in the new firm. Are there any benefits other than salary that I might not get elsewhere?

Having decided that it is time to go, or at least start looking round, it certainly would be wise to have a job lined-up before handing-in his notice. For Site Manager positions, the best place to start looking is employment agencies specialising in construction management jobs. There are loads of them about.

Agencies locate managers for the various firms and charge the new employers a fee (maybe ten to fifteen percent of the first years salary) for the service. (Site Managers won't be expected to pay any fee to the agency, and any agency seeking such a fee are probably breaking the law, and should be avoided.) The agency keeps details of managers in a database and when a new vacancy occurs and is notified to them, they search through the database to find a suitable candidate.

Many people wonder why construction firms would pay fees to agencies for recruitment of personnel. In reality when you calculate the cost of placing a decent advertisement in the newspapers, and add in the costs of interviewing a number of candidates, the fees charged by the agencies aren't that excessive.

Agencies normally operate in a fully confidential fashion. When you contact the agency they will usually ask you a lot of questions and may want to meet you in person for a chat. Next they will want a copy of your cv and if you don't already have one they will prepare one for you.

If they have suitable vacancies they will discuss these with you and if any of the jobs interests you, they will contact that firm and introduce you. If the employer is interested on the basis of your cv, then they may want to meet you for an interview. If not, the agency will send the cv of someone else on their books and so until the job is filled.

12.2.1 The Interview

When you are offered an interview as a result of recommendation by an agency it is reasonable to assume that the potential employer is interested in you. Recruitment and interviewing is a time consuming job, and employers won't waste their time interviewing someone just for the sake of it. So there is a reasonable chance you will get the job if you perform well at the interview stage. In other words – the job is yours to lose.

A few pointers for interviews:
- Be on time or ahead of time. If you don't know where the place is, go there the evening before and check it out unless it is a long way from you. If you can't do that, add at least

half an hour to your estimated journey time to find the place on the day.

- Tidy yourself up well for the interview. Scruffiness may be ok on site – but in an office at an interview it is not acceptable.
- Offer to shake hands with everyone on the panel. Make sure it is a good firm handshake.
- Maintain eye contact with anyone asking questions.
- Listen carefully to what is said – don't interrupt.
- Speak firmly and clearly – don't mumble and don't shout.
- Be prepared for the obvious questions – have your answers ready.
- If there are any obvious weaknesses in your cv, make sure you have answers ready to explain them away. These might include a number of jobs held in a short space of time i.e. "job-hopping."
- Try not to show desperation for the job – even if you are desperate.
- Don't say a bad word about past or current employers, or indeed anyone, at the interview – irrespective of your opinions.

12.2.2 Beware Of The Questions

Questions at job interviews operate on a number of levels, and replies given usually answer much more than the question asked.

One question that is always asked at an interview is "Why do you want to leave your present job?" or why "Why did you leave the last job?" This question operates on two levels. Firstly it's a straightforward *why* – what is the reason. But it also gives an insight to the psyche of the candidate. If you take the opportunity to explain all that is/was wrong with your current or last job you are telling just as much or maybe more about yourself and how you perform under pressure. If you list all the things that annoyed you about the current or last job, you may be perceived as a whinger or someone unable to handle pressure.

You could answer the question by saying that you felt it was time to move on – but this may project your image as that of someone who can't or won't settle, in a job and may go against you. Equally citing a personality clash may be read as *you* being difficult to get along with. So you see, the interviewee has to be very careful how questions are answered.

You could perhaps answer the question by saying that you don't talk about people behind their back, you were unhappy with the way the firm did things, and that while you don't want to be jumping from one job to another, you feel that a change might be best.

Another topic that will be raised is your salary expectations. You may be asked what salary you are currently on and you must proceed here with caution. If you don't have the use of a company vehicle in your current (last) job, you could 'throw one in' for the purposes of the interview. That way, the potential new employer may feel that he is going to have to match that, to interest you in the post. Be careful not to turn up in a company van, and at the same time tell the potential employer that you have a top of the range company car.

If you cite poor or inadequate salary as a reason for seeking a change, the interviewer might think he is entering into an auction with your current employers. He might decide that if he made an offer to you, that you would just use this offer as a bargaining chip in negotiations with your current employers, and might be put off by that prospect. So the whole issue of salary has to be handled skilfully, but skilful negotiations should be no problem to a Site Manager.

Other topics commonly covered include your experience and previous jobs you have held, how you might behave in specific situations. You might be asked about a job you were in ten years ago, not as a test of your powers of recall, but simply because it involved a construction process similar to one the firm is currently engaged in elsewhere. Or you might be asked how you would deal with trade unions, troublesome tradesmen or awkward clients.

12.2.3 Questions You Should Ask At The Interview

- How did the vacancy occur? It may be a simple case of expansion; the firm won a new job and didn't have personnel to cover it. If this is the case – what happens when the job is finished – last in – first out and all that. Or the last Site Manager may have been fired or left. This begs the question: *why*? You may need to probe that a bit to gain an insight into the real reasons, by the answer could be very relevant. Maybe they have unrealistic expectations, or are very difficult to please.

- What are the working hours of the firm? Will you be expected to work on Saturdays? If so, does this attract extra pay?

- Ask about their quality and Health & Safety policies. What is their accident record like? A higher than normal accident rate may indicate a culture of rushing on jobs or poor safety standards.

- How much work has the firm on their books?

- Ask any questions arising from the interview so far, or seek clarification of anything you don't understand.

12.3 So They Are Not Interested In You Then?

If you don't get the job – look on the bright side, maybe it just wasn't for you anyway. But don't let the entire experience be wasted. What went wrong? Carry out an assessment of the entire process – was there anything you could have handled better. Were you uncomfortable at the interview? If so, why? Was it something they asked that you weren't expecting? Was it the seating arrangements, the décor, or were you uncomfortable because you wanted to go to the bathroom? Were you late, or did you cut it so fine that you were not relaxed when the interview started? Did you ask for too much money, or did you sell yourself short?

Whatever your experience of an unsuccessful interview, a post-mortem should be carried out in the cold light of day, and there is no doubt that the experience of sitting the interview will stand to you when you face the next one.

If you were recommended by an employment agency, there is a good chance that your contact there will be able to tell you why you were unsuccessful. In fact it is likely that he will tell you things that the interviewers wouldn't. So ask him. And when he tells you, don't explode in his face or down the phone line to him, after all he is only telling you what he found out, not what he thinks. And if you get emotional, he won't be inclined to explain why you were unsuccessful a second time, in the unlikely event that that might occur.

12.4   So They Make An Offer

Well good, isn't it? Now you have to make up your mind. Is the offer attractive? If they offered you exactly what you asked for, was that because they felt that they wouldn't get you for any lower offer or are they desperate, or do you care either way?

You could discuss the offer with the agent if you were introduced through an agency. If not you could discuss it with a close friend, perhaps. There is little point in discussing it with anyone outside the industry as they won't be familiar with current pay rates, and won't know the companies involved.

I would advise against saying an instant "yes" to the offer. Think about it for a while. Carry out your analyses again, this time doing a direct comparison between your current job, if you have one, and the proposed one. Does it still seem as attractive? If it does and you are as sure as you can be, then go for it.

12.5   The Counter Offer

So you have said "yes" and you seek a meeting with your current employer to break the news – to hand in your notice. And then a complication arises – he makes an improved offer Great. Well no actually, because you have just told somebody else that you are about to join his firm. So you can't possibly accept the improved offer. Or can you?

Perhaps the best way to approach this would be to ask the proposed new employers to make you a written offer, and send you a copy of the proposed contract for you to look over. This will buy a little time, and while you are "looking-over" the contract you can hand in your notice. If the improved offer comes along and you decide to stay with your present employers, you could find something "unacceptable" in the proposed contract, but beware of the pitfalls of this tactic; the potential employers might offer to amend the contract to remove the "unacceptable" clause. So we are back to the skilled negotiating again. Just as well you are a Site Manager.

---THE END ---

Schedule 1 Typical Fás Safe Pass Register
To be updated as each new operative commences work on the site.

Name:	Date Commen-ced:	Fás Safe Pass Cert No:	Expiry Date of Cert:	Check-ed By:

Schedule 2 Pro Forma Minutes of Meeting

Item No:	Item:	Decision:	Follow-up Action By:

Schedule 3 Pro Forma Progress Report

| Task | Programme | | | Actual | | | Variation | Comments |
	Duration	Start	Complete	Duration	Start	Complete		

Schedule 4 - Who needs CSCS?

All construction workers undertaking the tasks listed in the Ninth schedule of the Construction Regulations, 2001 must have received training approved by FÁS under the Construction Skills Certification Scheme (CSCS) and be in possession of CSCS registration cards.

The list of tasks include

- Scaffolding – basic
- Scaffolding – advanced
- Tower crane operation
- Slinging/Signalling
- Telescopic Handler operations
- Tractor/Dozer operations
- Mobile Crane operation
- Crawler Crane operation
- Articulated Dumper operation
- Site Dumper operation
- 180° Excavator operation
- 360° Excavator operation
- Roof and Wall Cladding/Sheeting
- Built up Roof Felting

(Information on this page reproduced by kind permission of Health & Safety Authority)

Schedule 5 - List of Possible Topics For Tool Box Talks

1	Employee's Duties	26	Safe Use of Lifting Equipment
2	Site Housekeeping	27	Safe Use of Lifting Accessories
3	Clothing	28	Banksmen/Slingers
4	Eye Protection	29	Safe Use of Abrasive Wheels
5	Ear Protection	30	CSCS
6	Skin Protection	31	Vibration
7	Substance Abuse	32	Safe Use of Highly Flammable Liquids
8	Working at Heights	33	Safe Use of Compressed Gasses
9	Scaffolding	34	Leptospirosis (Weils Disease)
10	Mobile Tower Scaffolds	35	Safe Use of General Site Plant & Equipment
11	Ladder Use	36	Site Welfare
12	Working Platforms	37	Site Security
13	Roof Work	38	Dust & Fumes
14	Use of Hoists	39	Underground Services
15	Mobile Elevated Work Platforms	40	Road/Street Works
16	Use of Electricity	41	Accident Prevention
17	Safe Use of Portable Electrical Appliances	42	Safe Use of Chainsaws
18	Welding Operations	43	Safe Working Near Water
19	Manual Handling	44	Managing Site Waste
20	Safe Stacking on Site	45	Safety Representative
21	Safe Use of Cartridge Operated Tools	46	Preventing Pollution
22	Safe Use of Hand Tools	47	Accident Procedures
23	Fire Safety	48	Safe Working In Confined Spaces
24	Demolitions	49	Steelwork
25	Excavations	50	Recycling

Schedule 6 List of CR Forms
List of Forms for use with Safety, Health and Welfare at Work (Construction)Regulations (S.I. 481 of 2001) :

CR 1 Notification particulars - to be displayed on site and notified prior to commencement of work on a construction site.

CR 2 Excavator or loader used as crane - Certificate of safe working load.

CR 3 Crane - Certificate of test & examination.

CR 3A Crane - Report of anchoring/ballasting test.

CR 3B Crane - Report of automatic safe load indicator test.

CR 4 Crabs/Winches, Pulley blocks/Gin wheel - Certificate of test & examination.

CR 4A Lifting Appliances - Report of thorough examination (14 month intervals or after repair or before first use.)

CR 4B Lifting appliances/safe load indicators - Weekly Inspection report.

CR 5 Wire rope - Certificate of test & examination.

CR 6 Chains, slings, rings, links, hooks, plate clamps, shackles, swivels, eye bolts - Certificate of test & examination.

CR 6A Chains, Ropes and Lifting gear - Report of thorough examination.

CR 6B Chains, Ropes and Lifting gear - Report of annealing /heat treatment.

CR 7 Hoist - Certificate of test & examination.

CR 7A Hoists - Report of 6 -monthly thorough examination.

CR 7B Hoist to be used for carrying persons - Report of test & examination.

CR 7C Mobile Elevating Work Platform - Certificate of test & examination.

CR 7D Mobile Elevating Work Platform - Report of six-monthly thorough examination.

CR 8 Scaffolds - Report of inspection. *(Form discontinued – see working at height forms.)*

CR 9 Excavations, shafts, earthworks, underground works or tunnels, cofferdams & caissons - Report of thorough examination.

(These forms are published by, and available from: Health and Safety Authority, 10 Hogan Place, Dublin 2. Tel: 1890 289 389, Fax: 01-6147020, Email: wcu@hsa.ie)

(Information on this page reproduced by kind permission of Health & Safety Authority)

Published by Sionnach Media

Copyright © John Corless